THE DOCTRINE OF MAYA IN THE PHILOSOPHY OF THE VEDANTA

THE DOCTRINE OF MAYA IN THE PHILOSOPHY OF THE VEDANTA

PRABHU DUTT SHASTRI

Published by

Isha Books
B-63, Ist Floor
New Gupta Colony
Near DDA Market
Delhi - 110009

Distribution Network
gyanbooks.com
India, USA, Canada, UK, Australia

ISBN: 978-93-3311-357-1 (HB)

First Published, 1911

2nd Impression 2025

Printed at: Gyan Press, Delhi.

THE DOCTRINE OF MAYA IN THE PHILOSOPHY OF THE VEDANTA

Author: PRABHU DUTT SHASTRI

THE DOCTRINE OF MĀYĀ

In the Philosophy of the Vedānta

By

PRABHU DUTT SHĀSTRĪ

Ph.D. (Kiel), M.A., M.O.L., B.T. (Pb.), B.Sc. Lit. Hum. (Oxon.), of Christ Church, Oxford

Government of India Research Scholar (Sanskrit); Boden Research Grant, Oxford (1910); Theological Exhibitioner of Manchester College, Oxford; Member of the Oxford Philosophical Society; lately Associate of the Society for Psychical Research, London; Professor of Sanskrit, Oriental College, and First English Master and Lecturer in Psychology at the Government Training College, Lahore; Inspector and Examiner of Rishikula, Hardwar; etc., etc.

LONDON

LUZAC AND CO

(PUBLISHERS TO THE INDIA OFFICE)

46, GREAT RUSSELL STREET, W.C

1911

THE DOCTRINE OF MĀYĀ

In the Philosophy of the Vedanta

PRABHU DUTT SHASTRI

PREFACE

THE Doctrine of Māyā is the pivotal principle in the Advaita Philosophy—the final pronouncement of Indian speculation on the conception of Reality and Appearance. During the last thirty years a good deal has been written on the Vedānta, and naturally this doctrine has also been treated of, though only in passing and by the way. That it is richly supported in the later Vedānta is already an established fact, but a number of writers seem to conclude, rather hastily, that it is not the genuine product of the early speculation of the Upaniṣads, but has been later added to the original Vedānta by Śaṅkara and his followers. Some critics believe that it is imported from Buddhism and receives hardly any countenance from the Upaniṣads. The point is still debated, and it is only with a view to contribute a little towards a clearer understanding on this problem that I undertook to examine the Upaniṣads as minutely and as fully as I could, always relying upon the original texts more than the many more or less slipshod translations which are to be found. Hitherto these treatises have been looked upon as paradoxical, inconsistent and unsystematic. Scholars have only dashed at them to get out *some* meaning, but have hardly attempted to see if there existed in them an inner principle of unity and system. Deussen has, of course, indicated in his *Geschichte* the evolution of thought *within* the Upaniṣads, and has attempted to base their chronology on such internal evidence. Working independently on the original texts of the Upaniṣads, I have also reached practically the same conclusion, hence in Chapter II have enlarged and developed that scheme with the aid of all the more important passages bearing on each point. My method has been analytical, more appropriately synthetico-analytic; I have not stated a fact dogmatically, but have in every instance supported it with appropriate references, an examination of which will lead us inductively to the established conclusion. To those who do not hold the same view as I, a statement here and there may appear a little dogmatic, but that hardly touches me, since I have kept out all questions of personal belief and have only made an honest attempt to treat the question scientifically. To press one's own personal belief and point of view in a scientific inquiry vitiates, I believe, the conclusions to be arrived at.

On the question whether the conception of Māyā is found in the literature from Śaṅkara down to the present day, all opinions concur. The point to be investigated is how far and to what extent the conception is to be traced in the earlier literature before the time of Śaṅkara (who flourished about a thousand years before his spiritual disciple, Schopenhauer). Hence I have confined my inquiry to the Vedic literature, especially the Upaniṣads, and have carried my investigation down to Śaṅkara. My conclusions are (1) that the *conception* of Māyā is as old as some of the later books of the Ṛgveda where its forms are clearly noticeable, and that it gradually developed through the speculation of the Upaniṣads, and passing through the hands of Gauḍapāda and Śaṅkara was crystallized into a technical form, elaborated more and more as time went on; (2) that the *word* "Māyā," in the sense of "illusion" of course, occurs later—for the first time in the Śvetāśvatara Upaniṣad (iv. 10); and (3) that most of the critics of Māyā have started with gratuitously assuming Māyā to be a *concrete reality*, standing face to face with the Absolute as it were, a *tertium quid* between the Absolute and the Universe—and this has made their whole criticism futile and irrelevant. Some again have criticised it while perfectly ignoring one of its chief principles, which, expressed in modern Kantian phrase, would run: "The transcendental ideality of the world does not deprive it of its empirical reality."

Chapter I is more or less introductory, as it is intended to help indirectly towards a thorough grasp of the *idea* of Māyā. The philology of the word is not within the strict scope of my essay, but I have collected some suitable materials which may help to give an insight into the gradual transition of meaning of the word itself. In Chapter II I have attempted to trace the development of the *conception*, apart from the *word*. I do not, however, claim that the internal system of the Upaniṣads as sketched there, the transition of the various stages of thought, etc., is to be looked upon as an ultimate scheme or the only possible scheme. But surely it is *one* of the possible systematic ways of treating the Upaniṣads, consistent and coherent as far as it goes; and as yet I know of no better scheme. In the same chapter I have given a very brief analysis of Gauḍapāda's Kārikās on the Māṇḍūkya Upaniṣad, so far as they bear on the subject. This has its own justification, since the book is unfortunately not so well known, and even those who know it cursorily do not always understand it correctly. Some of its epigrammatic stanzas have been erroneously construed so as to countenance either the doctrine of Śūnyavāda or that of the reality of the world. I have selected the most typical as well as the most difficult passages, which, I may hope, will remove doubts on this point. It seems to me perfectly clear that Gauḍapāda was a thoroughgoing idealist and a worthy precursor of Śaṅkara. Then in Chapter III I have examined in brief the fundamental objections of the three other schools within the Vedānta, especially those of the Theistic Idealism of Rāmānuja. These objections have never before been collected together and discussed in reference to the doctrine of Māyā proper. The brevity in this part of the work was intended in order not to make the essay unnecessarily long. I had a mind, however, to append another chapter on the analogies of the *Conception of Māyā* in European philosophy, especially in the systems of Plato, Plotinus, Berkeley, Kant, and Schopenhauer. But in the present volume I have left it out, since it was felt that the present essay is in a way complete in itself, and that the additional part, which would have taken a considerable length in itself, is not necessary for the purpose.

I have given my own translation of passages which in my opinion have not been quite accurately rendered in the current translations. I have employed the words "appearance" and "illusion" rather indiscriminately in translating the word "māyā," though I am conscious of the subtle difference in the two conceptions. The word *illusion* has been most current in this connexion. Personally I would prefer the term *appearance*. The world, says the Māyā theory in its correct interpretation, is an *appearance*, not a *mere illusion*, since the latter as such is impossible. There are some passages where the latter conception seems to be held; e.g., "*māyāmātram*" if rendered as "a mere illusion" would imply this. But as I have shown in some detail with reference to passages from the Chāndogya Upaniṣad, this was not exactly what was meant by the old Indian thinkers. I hold that even if some of them really thought so, they were mistaken, and their ultra-rationalistic temper is to account for that. The Bṛhadāraṇyaka Upaniṣad emphatically proclaims that the Ātman is the only reality and that all plurality is a mere matter of words; the Chāndogya Upaniṣad, instead of starting with the Ātman, does so with the world, and comes to the same conclusion from this standpoint as well, viz., that *the world* is strictly speaking the Ātman itself, since there is no other existence but the Ātman. These two positions correspond to Schopenhauer's parallel sayings: (1) that the word is my "Vorstellung," (2) that it is my "Wille." As limited by space, time, and causality it is an *appearance*, but in its own nature it is the Ātman.

My best thanks are due to Professor Paul Deussen (Kiel), the Rev. Dr. J. Estlin Carpenter, Professor A. A. Macdonell and Professor J. A. Smith (Oxford), for their various useful suggestions. I am also grateful to Dr. F. H. Bradley, Dr. H. Rashdall, Dr. F. C. S. Schiller, Rev. L. P. Jacks (Oxford), Professor Henry Jones (Glasgow) and Professor Rudolf Eucken (Jena), who were kind enough to give me opportunities to discuss with them the subject of Māyā in the light of European philosophy in order to remove some of my difficulties. I have also to thank Dr. F. W. Thomas, Librarian, India

Office, Professor L. D. Barnett, of the British Museum, and the Librarians of the Bodleian for their kind assistance with books and unpublished manuscripts. To Professor Barnett I am further obliged for correcting the proof sheets.

PRABHU DUTT SHĀSTRĪ.

CHRIST CHURCH, OXFORD,
January, 1911.

CONTENTS

HISTORY OF THE WORD "MĀYĀ"

CHAPTER I

HISTORY OF THE WORD "MĀYĀ"

"MĀYĀ" is one of the most important and prominent words in the vocabulary of the Vedānta philosophy. If it had an unalterable and fixed meaning throughout the history of Indian thought, our task would have been lighter and we should have been saved the labour of writing this chapter. But as it is, the word is very fluid, and has at different times assumed various shapes of meaning. What it meant in the Vedic literature seems at first sight to be almost contradictory to its later connotation. Our present inquiry is intended to bring out the connecting links between its various meanings as they gradually passed through stages of transition. To avoid all subsequent error and confusion in understanding the conception of Māyā, it seems necessary to make clear the ground by first coming to terms with the word itself. The misconception and misuse of words is at the root of a host of fallacies; hence, we believe that no mean part of our task is finished if we are able, by means of a careful philological research, to define the concept of Māyā in brings out the same sense of "prajñā" while explaining "adhenvā carati māyayaiṣaḥ" (Nir. i. 6, 4),[1] "imām ū nu kavitamasya māyām" (Nir. vi. 3, 4),[2] "māyām ū tu yajñiyānām" (Nir. vii. 7, 5),[3] and "viśvā hi māyā avasi svadhāvaḥ" (Nir. xii. 2, 6).[4] We shall have occasion to see presently how far Sāyaṇa sticks to this meaning in his monumental commentary on R.V. Without citing any more lists of meanings, let us approach directly the Sanskrit literature—and the Vedas first—in order to judge the meaning correctly from the usage in the context.

After a careful examination of all the passages where the word occurs in any of its forms in the huge bulk of R.V., we arrive at the following conclusions :—

1. As regards frequency of occurrence the form most commonly met with is *māyāḥ*[5] (nom. and acc. pl.). It occurs no less than twenty-four times. Next in order comes *māyayā*[6] (instr. sing.), which

p. 134, l. 8 ; vol. iii., published 1886, p. 190, l. 2 ; p. 427, l. 10 ; vol. iv., p. 278, l. 10.

[1] Cf. Roth's ed. of *Yāska's "Nirukta,"* Göttingen, 1852 ; i. 20 (p. 39). R.V. x. 71. 5.

[2] Cf. Ibid. vi. 13 (p. 95–96). R.V. v. 85. 6.

[3] Cf. Ibid. vii. 27 (p. 124). R.V. x. 88. 6.

[4] Cf. Ibid. xii. 17 (p. 174). R.V. vi. 58. 1.

[5] Cf. R.V. i. 32. 4, 117. 3 ; ii. 11. 10, 27. 16 ; iii. 20. 3, 53. 8 ; v. 2. 9, 31. 7, 40. 6, 40. 8 ; vi. 18. 9, 20. 4, 22. 9, 44. 22, 45. 9, 58. 1 ; vii. 1. 10, 98. 5, 99. 4 ; viii. 41. 8 ; x. 53. 9, 73. 5, 99. 2, 111. 6.

[6] Cf. R.V. i. 80. 7, 144. 1, 160. 3 ; ii. 17. 5 ; iii. 27. 7 ;

occurs nineteen times; *māyinaḥ*[1] (acc. pl. and gen. sing. of *māyin*) occurs fifteen times; *māyābhiḥ*[2] (instr. pl.), thirteen times; *māyinam*[3] (acc. sing of *māyin*), ten times; the word *māyā*[4] itself three times, and each of the forms *māyām*[5] (acc. sing.), *māyī*[6] (nom. sing. of *māyin*), and *māyinām*[7] also occurs three times. *Māyinī* is found twice (R.V. v. 48. 1; x. 5. 3), and *māyinā* (instr. sing. of *māyin*) only *once* (R.V. vi. 63. 5). Other forms, including compounds, which occur once are *māyini* (R.V. v. 48. 3), *māyāvinā* (R.V. x. 24. 4), *māyāvān* (R.V. iv. 16. 9), *māyāvinam* (R.V. ii. 11. 9), and *māyāvinaḥ* (R.V. x. 83. 3).

2. There are altogether seventy-five hymns in R.V. in which the word appears in its simple or compound forms. Out of these thirty-five are addressed to Indra;[8] eight to Agni (R.V. i. 144;

iv. 30. 12, 30. 21; v. 63. 3, 63. 7; vi. 22. 6; vii. 104. 24; viii. 23. 15, 41. 3; ix. 73. 5, 73. 9, 83. 3; x. 71. 5; 85. 18, 177. 1.

[1] Cf. R.V. i. 39. 2, 51. 5, 54. 4, 64. 7, 159. 4; ii. 11. 10; iii. 38. 7, 38. 9, 56. 1; v. 44. 11; vi. 61. 3; vii. 82. 3; viii. 3. 19, 23. 14; x. 138. 3.

[2] Cf. R.V. i. 11. 7, 33. 10, 51. 5, 151. 9; iii. 34. 6, 60. 1; v. 30. 6, 44. 2, 78. 6; vi. 47. 18, 63. 5; viii. 14. 14; x. 147. 2.

[3] Cf. R.V. i. 11. 7, 53. 7, 56. 3, 80. 7; ii. 11. 5; v. 30. 6, 58. 2; vi. 48. 14; viii. 76. 1; x. 147. 2.

[4] Cf. R.V. iii. 61. 7; v. 63. 4; x. 54. 2.

[5] Cf. R.V. v. 85. 5, 85. 6; x. 88. 6.

[6] Cf. R.V. vii. 28. 4; x. 99. 10, 147. 5.

[7] Cf. R.V. i. 32. 4; iii. 20. 3, 34. 3.

[8] *Vide* R.V. i. 11, 32, 33, 51, 53, 54, 56, 80, 144, 160;

iii. 20, 27 ; v. 2 ; vii. 1 ; viii. 23 ; x. 5, 53) ; four to the Aśvins (R.V. i. 117 ; v. 78 ; vi. 63 ; x. 24) as well as to the Maruts (R.V. i. 39, 64 ; v. 58 ; vi. 48) ; three to Viśve-devāḥ (R.V. iii. 56 ; v. 44, 48) ; two each to Varuṇa (R.V. v. 85 ; viii. 41), Soma (R.V. ix. 73, 83), Mitrāvaruṇau (R.V. i. 151 ; v. 63), and Dyāvā-pṛthivyau (R.V. i. 100, 159) ; and one each to Uṣas (R.V. iii. 61), Sarasvatī (R.V. vi. 61), the Ādityas (R.V. ii. 27), Pūṣan (R.V. vi. 58), Atri (R.V. v. 40), Jñānam (R.V. x. 71), the Ṛbhus (R.V. iii. 60), Indrāvaruṇau (R.V. vii. 82), Somārkau (R.V. x. 85), Māyābheda (R.V. x. 177), Indrāviṣṇū (R.V. vii. 99) ; Prajāpati-Vaiśvāmitra (R.V. iii. 38), and Sūrya-vaiśvānarau (R.V. x. 88).

3. The word " Māyā " is not employed in one and the same sense throughout R.V. The Indian tradition itself bears ample testimony to this fact. As a rule, following Yāska, Sāyaṇa in most cases gives the meaning *prajñā*—i.e., energy, mental power as distinguished from physical—but he is not always definite ; in fact, he could not be so. It would be a gratuitous assumption on our part to expect the same word to be used in one and the same rigid sense by so many different Ṛṣis, who were by no means all contemporary. Tradition—as preserved in Sāyaṇa's commentary—tells us

ii. 11, 17 ; iii. 34, 53 ; iv. 16, 30 ; v. 30, 31 ; vi. 18, 20, 22, 44, 45, 47 ; vii. 28, 98, 104 ; viii. 3, 14, 76 ; x. 73, 99, 111, 138, 147.

that the two meanings *prajñā* and *kapaṭa*[1] are the most common, and sometimes run parallel. For instance, even in the very first hymn (R.V. i. 11. 7), in which the word appears as *māyābhiḥ* (and *māyinam*), Sāyaṇa seems to waver between these two meanings, and leaves the reader to make his own choice. He explains *māyābhiḥ* by *kapaṭaviśeṣaiḥ* (lit. "by special stratagems, artifices") but adds at the same time that it may also mean "prajñābhiḥ" ("by wondrous powers," Griffith). Wilson adopts the first meaning, "by stratagems," Ludwig[2] translates it as "durch übernatürliche Kraft." Rosen[3] also renders it as "praestigiis." But these are not the only meanings accepted by tradition. In R.V. iii. 27. 7 Sāyaṇa explains "*māyayā*" by *karmaviṣayābhijñānena*,"[4] i.e., "by *knowledge* of sacred rites." This meaning appears to us to be rather far-fetched. In R.V. iii. 60. 1 he renders the same word as *karmabhiḥ*.[5] In iii. 61. 7, *māyā* is translated as "power," "glory"—"prabhārūpā," lit. in the form of effulgence or light. In R.V.

[1] Which mean artifice, deception, cunning. Germ. List, Betrug, Kunst, Kraft, etc.

[2] Ludwig, *Der Rigveda*. Prag, 1878.

[3] Fridericus Rosen, *Rigveda-Samhitā*, Liber Primus, Sanskritè et Latinè, London, 1838.

[4] Sāyaṇa derives this meaning thus: mimīte jānīte karma mīyate anayeti vā māyā karmaviṣayajñānam (root mā, to know), 3rd conj. *mimīte*, or mā, to measure, *mīyate*.

[5] Sāyaṇa adds: mīyante jñāyanta' iti māyāḥ karmaṇi. Cf. also R.V. x. 53. 9, where Sāyaṇa says: "Karmanāmaitat."

iv. 30. 21, and v. 30. 6, Sāyaṇa emphatically gives the meaning *śakti* (power).

Again, keeping aside for a moment Maṇḍalas i. and x. of R.V.—which are now supposed on good evidence to have been subsequently added to the original collection—we find the same want of fixity of the meaning conveyed by the term in the other books of R.V. For instance, according to Sāyaṇa's tradition the word is used in the sense of "deception" in R.V. ii. 11. 10, iii. 34. 6, iv. 16. 9, vi. 20. 4, vii. 104. 24, and so forth, while both the meanings "power" and "deception" are taken in v. 30. 6 simultaneously. In v. 31. 7 the word is taken to mean "a young woman." This meaning too has its own justification and is not unconnected with the other two meanings. In what sense a woman can be called *māyā* is not to be discussed here, but will find its appropriate place in the sequel.

The two chief meanings, therefore, which the word is assigned in R.V. are "power" (Prajñā, lit. "knowledge") and "deception" ("Kapaṭa,' Vañcanā). The above examination of the various passages in which the word occurs has shown us that wherever it means "power" the idea of "*mystery*" necessarily goes with it; i.e., it does not mean any "physical" power, but "a mysterious power of the *will*," which we would translate into such Sanskrit expressions as *saṅkalpa-śakti* or *icchā-śakti*. In R.V. iii. 53. 8, for instance, Indra is spoken of as "assuming many different forms," and it is not done by his "physical" power but simply by his wonderful and extraordinary "will-power" (anekarūpagrahaṇasāmarthya). He *wills* that he may assume such and such forms and it is realized; hence Indra is very frequently termed *māyin* in the Vedic hymns. Certain mysterious things or results are produced by this mysterious will-power, and these results being *extra*-ordinary by their very nature may be said to set at naught the ordinary human understanding, which because of its inherent limitations is apt to be "deceived" by such phenomena. Hence, the idea of "mystery" being common to both these meanings, it is quite easy to understand the transition from the idea of "mysterious will-power" to that of "deception." In fact the two ideas interpenetrate each other, so much so that it seems to us rather a forced distinction to make when we speak of the transition. Still, distinctions *are* to be made, especially when they help us to a clearer understanding of that which is really beyond them.

We may, however, note here in passing that where Indra is spoken of as assuming various forms (cf. especially iii. 53. 8 and vi. 47. 18) it appears that the singers of the hymns—and Indians of the Vedic age in general—were not unaware of a distinction between the one and the many, of the possibility of the one becoming the many and of the latter being a deceptive creation of a mysterious power.

This inference seems to us to be reasonable and valid. The fact is very important, as we shall have the opportunity to speak more of it later. Here we cannot do anything more than simply mention it, since we are now concerned only with the meanings of the word so far as it can be determined by a collocation of ancient texts in a more or less chronological order.

Now, the word does not so often occur in the Yajurveda and the Sāmaveda. This cannot surprise us in any way. These two Vedas contain mostly the mantras of the Ṛgveda—which are adapted and arranged to suit their particular functions—as well as some new mantras. In the Y.V. all ideas are subservient to sacrifice (yajña) and its various elaborate ceremonies; while in the S.V. chanting or singing the mantras is the chief function.

The R.V. is the chief source of these two Vedas, which along with it form what is known as "trayī vidyā," i.e., triple knowledge. The comparative absence of the word *Māyā* from the Y.V. and the S.V. does not affect our examination, as the R.V. can be safely taken to be an index to the ideas and views of the ancient Indians of that age. It was not very long before these two Vedas sprang into existence, to be ranked with the R.V. as to their importance and authority in the tradition of the Āryans. In fact these three Vedas seem to have been brought into existence almost simultaneously, though it must be admitted that it took a considerably long interval of time to give them the shape in which they are found at present, i.e., as a complete set of books.

The Atharva-Veda was added to the *trayī-vidyā* much later. The fact has been amply proved by a critical examination of both external and internal evidence. It is not for us to enter into the question here. The A.V. represents a different state of civilization of society from that described in the R.V. And we are satisfied to note that the word Māyā is not missing in it. Altogether the word occurs in ten books only, in sixteen hymns [1] and twenty times in all (in A.V. viii. 9. 5 and viii. 10. 22 the word occurring twice in each of the hymns and twice also in xiii. 2 and xix. 27).

The form *māyā* occurs only *once* (A.V. viii. 9. 5). The instrumental singular, *māyayā*, occurs most frequently, viz., eight times. [2] *Māyinaḥ* [3] occurs three times and *māyām* [4] and *māyāḥ* [5] twice each. Other forms which occur only once are *māye* (viii. 10. 22), *māyāyāḥ* (viii. 9. 5), *māyābhiḥ* (xii. 1. 8) and *māyī* (v. 11. 4).

[1] A.V. ii. 29. 6; iv. 23. 5, 38. 3; v. 11. 4; vi. 72. 1; vii. 81. 1; viii. 3. 24, 4. 24, 9. 5, 10. 22; x. 8. 34; xii. 1. 8. xiii. 2. 3, 2. 11; xix. 27. 5, 27. 6, 66. 1, 68. 1. Cf. Whitney's *Index Verborum to the Published Text of the Atharva-Veda*, New-Haven, JAOS. vol. xii. p. 225.

[2] A.V. iv. 38. 3; vi. 72. 1; vii. 81. 1; viii. 4. 24; x. 8. 34; xiii. 2. 3, 2. 11; xix. 68. 1.

[3] A.V. xix. 27. 5, 27. 6, 66. 1.

[4] A.V. ii. 29. 6; viii. 10. 22.

[5] A.V. iv. 23. 5; viii. 3. 24.

From the very nature of the contents of the Atharva-Veda it is easy to judge the meaning of the word *māyā* as used in it. Here the mysterious or magical element of the "power" spoken of in the Ṛgveda is more emphasized, and there hardly seems any scope for doubting the meaning. It means "magic" throughout, and is even translated as "illusion" (the great controversial word in our subject) by Whitney.[1] The two passages in which it is rendered so are found in the well-known "Mystic" hymn, extolling the Virāj, e.g., in A.V., 10. 22, "The Asuras called to her, O Illusion[2] (māyā), come!" It may also be stated, by the way, that A.V. vii. 81. 1, viii. 3. 24, viii. 4. 24 are taken from R.V. x. 85. 18, v. 2. 9, vii. 10. 4 respectively.

Now we have seen so far that *māyā* in R.V. means "a wondrous or supernatural power," "an extraordinary skill," and that the "supernatural" element is more strongly emphasized in A.V., where it means "magic" and hence "illusion."

With regard to the word occurring in the Brāhmaṇas it would be useless for us to enter into any

[1] Cf. *Atharva-Veda Samhitā*, trans. by W. D. Whitney (Harvard Oriental Series), 1905, vol. ii. p. 507, 514. For translation see also *Les Livres viii, et ix. de L'Atharva Véda Traduits et Commentés*, par Victor Henry, Paris, 1894; and Griffith's *The Hymns of the Atharva-Veda*, and Ludwig's *Der Rigveda*, Band iii., Einleitung, Prag, 1878, p. 493.

[2] We would rather say "mystery" instead of Whitney's use of the word "illusion" here.

details here. The really philosophical treatises, which are of fundamental importance for our purpose, are the final portions of the Brāhmaṇas, called the Upaniṣads. But before we take up the Upaniṣads proper, we may quote a few references from the Brāhmaṇas too in the way of *Sthālī-pulāka-nyāya.*[1]

The Vājasaneyī-Samhitā [2] contains the forms māyā (xi. 69), māyām,[3] māyayā [4] and māyāyām,[5] and Mahīdhara in his commentary gives the words "prajñā" and "buddhi" as synonyms of "māyā." The Aitareya Brāhmaṇa [6] has māyayā (vi. 36), māyām, māyāvant, and māyāvattaraḥ (viii. 23), where the word clearly means "supernatural or magical skill." The form "māyayā" also occurs in the Taittirīya Brāhmaṇa [7] (iii. 10. 8. 2) where,

[1] i.e., the maxim of "the cooking-pot and the boiling rice." By finding one grain well-cooked we infer the same with regard to all the others. So the conditions of the class may be inferred from that of a part, if the whole is made up of homogeneous and similar parts. Cf. Patañjali's Mahābhāṣya, i. 4. 23 (Vārt. 15). "Paryāpto hi ekaḥ pulakaḥ sthālyā nidarśanāya."

[2] Weber, *The White Yajurveda*, part I, The Vājasaneyī-Samhitā, in the Mādhyandina and the Kāṇva-Śākhā, with the commentary of Mahīdhara. Berlin and London, 1852.

[3] Ibid., p. 420. V.S. xiii. 44. Mahīdhara adds, "*mīyate jñāyate anayā iti māyā.*"

[4] Ibid., p. 728, V.S. xxiii. 52.

[5] Ibid., p. 841, V.S. xxx. 7.

[6] *Das Aitareya Brāhmaṇa*, herausgegeben von Theodor Aufrecht, Bonn, 1879. See p. 184 and 230.

[7] *The Taittirīya Brāhmaṇa of the Black Yajurveda,*

as Sāyaṇa also adds, it means "by divine power." Further the Śatapatha-Brāhmaṇa [1] too contains the forms "māyām (ii. 4. 25), and "māye" (iii. 2. 4. 1), māyāvant (xiii. 5. 4. 12) where the word means "supernatural power." [2] The Pañcaviṁśatī Brāhmaṇa also has the word māyayā (xiii. 6. 9) in the same sense. Māyāvant (as an adj.) is seen in Ait. Br. viii. 23, and in Śat. Br. xiii. 5. 4. 12. These typical examples are more than sufficient for our purpose, and we now hasten to quote references from the Upaniṣads and from the Bhagavadgītā, which may be termed the final Upaniṣad or the kernel of all the Upaniṣads.[3]

The Bṛhadāraṇyaka Upaniṣad, the oldest as well as the most important in many ways, contains the word "māyābhiḥ" (ii. 5. 19),[4] the Praśṇa Up.

with the Commentary of Sāyana, ed. by Rajendra Lala Mitra, Calcutta, 1859, vol. iii. p. 237.

[1] *The Śatapatha Brāhmana of the White Yajurveda*, with Sāyaṇa's Com., ed. by Ācārya Satyavrata Sāmaśramī ; vol. ii., Kāṇḍa II, Calcutta, 1906, p. 191, and vol. iii, Kāṇḍa III, Calcutta, 1905, p. 119 (Bibl. Ind.).

[2] Sāyaṇa translates māyā here as "Aghaṭita-ghaṭanā-śaktiḥ," and in the next passage expresses the same idea by "paramavyāmohakāriṇī śaktiḥ." These synonyms give a clear explanation.

[3] See G. A. Jacob, *Concordance to the Principal Upaniṣads and Bhagavadgītā.*

[4] This is the famous quotation from R.V. vi. 47. 18, which also occurs in Śat. Br. xiv. 5. 5. 19 ; also in Jaiminīya-Upaniṣad Br. i. 44. 1. See *Bṛhadāraṇyakopaniṣad*, herausgegeben und übersetzt von O. Böhtlingk, St. Petersburg, 1889, p. 22.

māyā (i. 16),[1] the Śvetāśvatara Up. māyā (i. 10),[2] māyām, māyinam (iv. 10), [3] māyī,[4] and māyayā (iv. 9).

Among the later Upaniṣads too the word occurs; the forms māyā, māyām, māyayā in Nṛp. Up. (iii. 1; v. 1) [5] and in Nṛut. Up. (Khaṇḍa 9), [5] māyāmātram in Nṛut. Up. (1 and 5). [5] In Cūl. Up. (3) [6] we read—

---

[1] Bibl. Indic. vol. viii. No. 29. Here Māyā is spoken of as a defect along with *jihmam* (moral crookedness) and *anṛtam* (telling a lie). It is itself mithyācārarūpadoṣa (the defect of hypocrisy).

[2] Here māyā means the great cosmic illusion. In his com. on the passage Śaṇkara adds, "sukhaduḥkhamohātmakaśeṣaprapañcarūpamāyā," i.e., the whole world as a sum-total of pleasure, pain, delusion, etc.

[3] Here the Prakṛti of the Sāṇkhya is spoken of as *māyā*. Cf. "māyām tu prakṛtim viddhi māyinam tu maheśvaram."

[4] The Great Lord is called *māyī* here and in the following stanza. He is said to create the universe only by his māyā-śakti.

[5] "The Nṛsiṁha-Tāpanī Upaniṣad," Bibl. Indica, Cal., 1871. As these and other minor Upaniṣads are not easily available we give the following quotations in full: "Māyā vā eṣā nārasiṃhī," "nātmānaṃ māyā spṛśati," "Kṣetram kṣetram vā māyaiṣā sampadyate," "māyā ca tamorūpānubhūteḥ," "evam evaiṣā māyā," "māyā cāvidyā ca svayam eva bhavati," "māyām etāṃ śaktiṃ vidyāt," "ya etāni māyāṃ śaktiṃ veda," "māyayā vā etat sarvam veṣṭitam," "māyayā vahirveṣṭitam," "māyayā hy anyad iva," "mūḍha iva vyavaharann āste māyayaiva," "māyayā nāsamvittiḥ svaprakāśe," "trayam apy etat (and trayam atrāpi) suṣuptam svapnam māyāmātram," (Nṛut 1), "idam sarvam yad ayam ātmā māyāmātram" (Nṛut. 5).

[6] For Cūlikā and other Upaniṣads see the Collection of

"Vikārajananīm *māyām* aṣṭarūpām ajām dhruvam,"

where Māyā is spoken of as bringing about the existence of the phenomenal world.

The Sarv. Up.[1] reads—

"Katham pratyagātmā paramātmā ātmā *māyā* ceti," [2]

where an inquiry is made into the meanings of these four terms including māyā, and the answer is given in section 4:—

"Anādir antarvatnī pramāṇāpramāṇasādhāraṇā na satī nāsatī na sadasatī svayam avikārād vikārahetau nirūpyamāṇe asatī, anirūpyamāṇe satī lakṣaṇaśūnyā sā māyety ucyate,"

where the mysterious nature of māyā is described.

The Rāmap. Up.,[3] which is one of the sectarian Upaniṣads, speaking of Rāma and Sītā as Prakṛti and Puruṣa, reads thus—

"tato Rāmo mānavo māyayādhyāt" (17).
"koṇapārśve ramāmāye" (61).

thirty-two Upaniṣads, published by the Ānandāśrama Sanskrit Series, No. 29, Poona, 1895. The Cūl. Up. contains only twenty-one ślokas, divided into two khaṇḍas, and belongs to A.V., p. 230.

1 *The Sarvopaniṣatsāra* is a small prose-treatise containing only five sections, in the last of which it gives a good description of māyā. See Ibid., p. 587–92.

2 The Great Lord is called mayī here and in the following stanza. He is said to create the universe only by his māyā-śakti.

3 The Rāmapūrvatāpanīya Up. contains ninety-four ślokas divided into ten khaṇḍas. See ibid., pp. 487–529.

"māyāvidye ye kalāpāratattve" (89).
"namo māyāmayāya ca" (30).

The Gopīcandana Up. reads—

"māyāsahitabrahmasambhogavaśāt" (4).
"māyāśabalitam Brahmāsit" (Ibid.).

The Kṛṣṇa Up. also reads—

"māya sā trividhā proktā (5).
"māyā tredhā hy udāhṛtā" (6).
"ajayyā Vaiṣṇavī māyā" (7).
"Hariḥ sākṣān māyāvigrahadhāraṇaḥ" (11).
"Māyayā mohitaṃ jagat" (12).
"tasya māyā jagat katham" (13).

In all these passages *māyā* means "appearance," "illusion,"[1] etc. The same sense is further found in "sa evam māyāparimohitātmā" (Kaivalya Up. 12), and "indrajālam iva māyāmayam" (Maitri Up. iv. 2).

One of the most brilliant and important works on Advaitism is Gauḍapāda's Kārikās on the Māṇḍūkya Upaniṣad.[2] These are divided into four parts (prakaraṇas): (1) Āgama; (2) Vaitathya; (3) Advaita; (4) Alāta-śānti, each of which is regarded as a separate Upaniṣad. Of the subject-matter of this important work we shall have occasion to speak in Chapter II. But here we may only point

[1] We are consciously using these two words as synonyms here.

[2] The Māṇḍūkya-Upaniṣad (of A.V.) with Gauḍapāda's Kārikās, together with Śaṅkara's Comm., Ānandāśrama Series, No. 10, 1890, Poona.

out that the word "māyā" is here also used in the same sense of "appearance," "illusion." (In one passage, however, it means "supernatural power," ii. 12.)

The Kārikā contains sixteen passages altogether in which the word *māyā* occurs. Out of these, Part III contributes no less than six passages, Part IV contributing four, and each of the other two parts contributing three,

"svapnamāyāsarūpeti sṛṣṭir anyair vikalpitā,"

where the world is likened to a world of dreams and to illusion, both of which are false.

"anādimāyayā supto yadā jīvaḥ prabudhyate" (i. 16),

where the cosmic illusion—under the influence of which the individual feels as if "asleep"—is spoken of as beginningless.

"Māyāmātram idam dvaitam advaitam paramārthataḥ" (i. 17),

where the duality, i.e., the multiplicity of which the word is composed, is declared mere illusion.

"Kalpayaty ātmanātmānam ātmā devaḥ svamāyayā" (ii. 12),

where *māyā* is said to be the Lord's own "wondrous power." Here the sense of such a supernatural power is maintained. But, as will be shown presently, the two ideas are closely allied to each other. The sense of "illusion" is a natural development of the idea of such a "power."

> "māyaiṣā tasya devasya yayā sammohitaḥ svayam" (ii. 19),

where māyā is spoken of as the Lord's great illusion.

> "svapnamāye yathā dṛṣṭe gandharvanagaraṃ yathā" (ii. 31),

where again *māyā* is collated with *svapna,* and it is said that the waking world has no substantiality, like a dreaming world or like a "fata morgana."

> "saṃghātāḥ svapnavat sarve ātmamāyāvisarjitāḥ" (iii. 10),

where the so-called objective existences in this world are declared false and mere creations of the Ātman's *māyā* (*avidyā*).

> "māyayā bhidyate hy etan nānyathājaṃ kathaṃcana" (iii. 19),

where the differences or the plurality are said to be due to mere illusion. The same thought is repeated in

> "neha nāneti cāmnāyād indro māyābhir ity api
> ajāyamāno bahudhā māyayā jāyate tu saḥ" (iii. 24).

Further, in the following two passages it is discussed how the world is created not from *not-being* but from *being*—not "in reality" but "as it were":—

> "sato hi māyayā janma yujyate na tu tattvataḥ" (iii. 27).
> "asato māyayā janma tattvato naiva yujyate" (iii. 28).

In Part IV we find—

"Upalambhāt samācārān māyāhastī yathocyate" (iv. 44),

where the empirical existence of the world is granted like the one granted to an illusive elephant.

"janma māyopamaṃ teṣāṃ sā ca māyā na vidyate" (iii. 58),

where "māyā" is said to have no real existence at all.

"yathā māyāmayād vījāj jāyate tanmayo 'ṅkuraḥ" (iv. 59),

where the creation, destruction, etc., of the worldly objects is described as *māyā*, an appearance, seeming true only in the realm of appearance.

"yathā svapne dvayābhāsaṃ cittaṃ calati māyayā,
tathā jāgrad dvayābhāsaṃ cittaṃ calati māyayā" (iv. 61),

where the seeming duality is spoken of as mere *vijñānamaya*, and the waking and the dreaming states are compared in this regard.

The same sense is observed in the great epic, the Mahābhārata. For instance—

"purā vikurute māyām" (i. 6,029).
Cf. also i. 7,631, iii. 2,557, xiii. 7,595,
"māyām mohinīm samupāśritāḥ" (i. 1,156),
"apsarā devakanyā vā māyā" (iii. 15,580).

Now we come to the Bhagavadgītā, which is the finest gem in our New Testament of the Upaniṣads, and which contains the essentials of all our philosophy.

"prakṛtiṃ svām adhiṣṭhāya
sambhavāmy ātmamāyayā" (iv. 6).

Here it means "will-power."

"Daivī hy eṣā guṇamayī
mama *māyā* duratyayā,
mām eva ye prapadyante
māyām etāṃ taranti te" (vii. 14).

Here it means "illusion," which being dependent on God is spoken of as "divine."

"*māyayā*pahṛtajñānā
āsuram bhāvam āśritāḥ" (vii. 15).

Here, too, the same sense of "illusion."

"bhrāmayan sarvabhūtāni
yantrārūḍhāni *māyāyā*" (xviii. 61).

Here, too, it means the great "illusive Power."

Now let us turn to the *System* of the Vedānta, properly so called as one of the six systems or schools of Indian philosophy. The Sūtras (aphorisms, condensed formulas) which constitute this system are called the *Brahma-Sūtras* or the *Vedānta-Sūtras*, and are 555 in number. The *word māyā*, however, occurs only in one of these (iii. 2. 3), which runs thus—

"Māyāmātram tu kārtsnyena anabhivyaktasvarūpatvāt"[1]

where, speaking of the nature of a dream, the dream-world is pronounced to be mere "illusion." Max

[1] Cf. Deussen, *Die Sūtras des Vedānta*, Leipzig, 1887, p. 504; Thibaut, *Vedānta-Sūtras*, Part II (vol. xxxviii. of S.B.E.), Clarendon Press, Oxford, 1896, p. 134.

Müller[1] seems to be incorrect when he says that the word "need not mean more than a *dream.*" In that case the sūtra would mean that the dream-world is a dream, which hardly has any sense. Doubtless the word means "*illusion*" here, as it is quite in keeping with the spirit of the preceding two sūtras, which also bear on the same subject of the unreality of the dream-world.

The most important, authoritative and popular, as well as the oldest, commentary on the Vedānta-Sūtras is the one by *Śaṅkara* (otherwise called Śaṅkarācārya) called the "Śārīraka-Bhāṣya." This Bhāṣya has so much been respected that it forms a part and parcel of the technical system of the Vedānta together with the Sūtras. Of the intrinsic merit of Śaṅkara's commentary or of its relation to the Brahma-Sūtras we shall have occasion to speak later on. Suffice it to say here that the term "māyā" is found in the commentary fifteen times in the following passages,[2] and it invariably has the sense of "illusion."

1. "yathā *māyāvinaś* carma-khaḍgadharāt sūtreṇa ākāśam adhirohataḥ sa eva *māyāvī* paramārtharūpo bhūmiṣṭho 'nyaḥ" [3] (On i. 1. 17.)

[1] Max Müller, *The Six Systems of Indian Philosophy*, Longmans, 1899, p. 243.

[2] We have selected here the more typical and important passages. No doubt there are some others too, some of these having been quoted in ch. ii.

[3] Śaṅkara's Comm. on l. 1. 17. p. 120, l. 16 of the Vedānta-Sūtras, Bibl. Ind., Cal., 1863.

Here the word "*māyāvin*" occurs and means a "juggler"; so too it means in the following—

2. "eka eva parameśvaraḥ kūṭastha-nityo vijñānadhātur avidyayā *māyayā* māyāvivad anekadhā vibhāvyate." [1] (On i. 3. 19).
3. "māyāmayī mahā-suṣuptiḥ." (On i. 4. 3.)[2]
4. "Kvacin māyā iti sūcitam." (Ibid.)[3]
5. "Avyaktā hi sā māyā." (Ibid.)[4]
6. "Māyāvī iva māyāyāḥ prasāritasya jagataḥ." (On ii. 1. 1.)[5]
7. "yathā svayam prasāritayā māyayā māyāvi triṣv api kāleṣu na samspṛśyate avastutvāt, evam paramātmāpi samsāra-māyayā na samspṛśyate iti," etc. (On ii. 1. 9).[6]
8. "māyāmātraṃ hi etat." (Ibid.) [7]
9. "yathā ca māyāvī svayam-prasāritām māyāṃ icchayā anāyāsena eva upasamharati." (On ii. 1. 21.) [8]
10. "loke 'pi devādiṣu māyāvi-ādiṣu ca svarūpa-anumardena eva vicitrā hasti-aśva-ādi sṛṣṭayo dṛśyante." (On ii. 1. 28).[9]

These are the ten passages in Śaṅkara's Bhāṣya in which the word occurs. It is possible to discover more passages in the same on a minuter analysis of the vast and voluminous commentary, but that would not affect our problem in any way. It is

1 Śaṅkara on I. 3. 19. Ibid., p. 269, ll. 1–3.
2 Ibid., p. 342, l. 9.
3 Ibid., p. 342, l. 12.
4 Ibid., p. 343, l. 1.
5 Śaṅkara on i. 3. 19, Ibid., p. 406, l. 6.
6 Ibid., p. 432, ll. 8–10.
7 Ibid., p. 432, l. 13.
8 Ibid., p. 472, l. 9.
9 Ibid., p. 484, l. 11.

true beyond doubt that Śaṅkara means by māyā nothing but "illusion."

From Śaṅkara's time downward the phraseology of the Vedānta was more and more settled technically, and even modern writers on the Vedānta use the word "māyā" in the same sense of "illusion" which was so clearly brought out by Śaṅkara. After his time there has not been any desire to change the meaning of the term by a different usage. Hence it will hardly be of much use to examine the later Sanskrit texts on the Vedānta in order to find out the word "māyā." In the first place, it is exceedingly difficult to do so, since the later literature is so varied, vast and undefined in extent; secondly, the later Vedānta is in many cases mixed with the ideas of the Sāṅkhya, Buddhism, etc.; and thirdly, even if we were to succeed in collecting all the more important modern works on pure Vedānta and were to collate the passages containing "māyā" in a similar way, it would scarcely be of any profit, since, as we have already said, the modern usage of the term is in no way different from that of Śaṅkara. A glance through such works as the *Pancadaśī*, the *Vedāntasāra*, the *Vedāntaparibhāṣā*, the *Ātmabodha*, the *Vivekacūḍāmaṇi*, etc., will amply endorse this fact. We may, therefore, safely close our survey of the meanings of the term when we have come down to Śaṅkara's time.

Apart from its philosophic use, the word "māyā" is used in modern classical Sanskrit to convey some other ideas also. Sometimes it means "a female juggler."[1] Again it means "deception" or fraud (kapaṭa) or hypocrisy (chadma), e.g., in the Mahābhārata.

"sevetām amāyayā gurum" (xiii. 7,595).

i.e., "let both of them serve the teacher without any deception."

It also means "illusion" in an "unphilosophical" sense, i.e., in an ordinary way free from the technical shade of the philosophical idea. For example, in the Raghuvamśa we read—

"māyām mayodbhāvya parīkṣito 'si" (ii. 62),

i.e., you have been tested by me creating "illusion."

The word is also used sometimes as a proper name. Buddha's mother was called "māyā" (full name: "māyā Devī"), as "māyādevīsuta" is one of Buddha's names mentioned in the "Amarakośa."[2]

[1] Cf. *Amarakośa* (*Dictionary of the Sanskrit Language*, by Amara Simha), edited with an English interpretation and annotations by H. T. Colebrooke, Serampur, 1808, p. 241, Śloka 11: "syān māyā śāmbarī māyākāras tu prātihārikaḥ."

[2] *Amarakośa*, ed. Colebrooke, Ibid. p. 3, Śloka 10: "Gautamaś ca-arkabandhuś ca māyādevīsutaś ca saḥ." Cf. also Max Müller's *Six Systems of Indian Philosophy*, Longmans, Green & Co., 1899, p. 122. See also "maya" in Wilson's *Dictionary in Sanskrit and English*, second enlarged edition, Calcutta, 1832, p. 657; also *Sanskrit Dictionary*, by Tārānatha Tarkavācaspati, Calcutta, 1882; *Padmacandrakośa*, by Prof. Ganesh Datta Shastri, Nirṇaya-sāgara

Even at the present day in India some girls are actually named "Māyā-Devī" or "Māyā-vatī" or "Māyā-Kaur." The chief reason why they are so named is that they are looked upon as auspicious if their name means "wealth" or "a bringer of wealth," etc., everything bearing on wealth being supposed to be auspicious. In India almost all names mean something definite—most of them are after the designations of some gods or goddesses. It is supposed that if a girl is named "māyā" she will ever be abounding in riches. This idea of "riches" leads us to the next meaning of the word, which is the goddess of wealth, called "Lakṣmī." Lakṣmī is the presiding deity of wealth, and her presence is always desired by the Hindus.[1] It also means sometimes mere "wealth." This is especially noticed in modern works in Hindi and Punjābī.

In the Sāṅkhya system Māyā is identified with

Press, Bombay; further see F. Bopp, *Glossarium Sanscritum*, Berolini, 1847, p. 263; Macdonell, *Sanskrit English Dictionary*, Lond., 1893, p. 226; Theodore Benfrey, *A Sanskrit English Dictionary*, Lond., 1866, p. 701, etc., etc.

[1] Every year in the month of Āśvina there is a special festival observed called the Dīpamālā (lit. a row of lamps), as on that day every Hindu burns a number of lamps (generally of clay) arranged in long rows in all parts of his house, especially on the outside. A special traditional story of Lakṣmī is recited, and it is hoped that the goddess of wealth will come to all those who love light (prakāśa) and not darkness.

Prakṛti (the primordial "matter") as the source of the universe, with the distinct difference that the latter is *real*. It is the equilibrium of the three qualities of Sattva, Rajas and Tamas.[1] It is also called *Pradhāna*. It has a real and independent existence and brings about the evolution of the whole world in company with the Puruṣa. In other words, the Sāṅkhya system is based on an out-and-out dualism. This dualism is questioned and finally solved by the Vedānta in so far as the Prakṛti is transformed into Māyā, and the Puruṣa into Brahman, and so the mutual opposition of the two is destroyed.

The word "Māyā" is derived from √mā, to measure—"mīyate anayā iti," i.e., by which is measured, meaning thereby, as tradition has it, that illusive projection of the world by which the immeasurable Brahman appears as if measured. The same root gives further the sense of "to build," leading to the idea of "appearance" or illusion. Sāyaṇa,[2] in his commentary on R.V. i. 11. 7, too derives the word from "*māḍ* māne" (i.e., √mā, to measure). Further on, while explaining the form "māyayā" in R.V. iii. 27. 7 he derives it from √*mā*, to know, or to measure, and adds—"mimīte jānīte karma mīyate anayeti vā māyā karmaviṣayābhijñānam," i.e., (1) √Mā, to know—by which the ritual,

[1] "Sattva-rajas-tamasām sāmyāvasthā prakṛtiḥ."

[2] For the derivations proposed by Sāyaṇa see also above, p. 8.

etc., are known, (2) √Mā, to measure—by which the ritual, etc., are measured (i.e., understood, or performed); hence māyā = the knowledge of the object of the ritual, etc.

Again in R.V. iii. 60. 1 also, adds Sāyaṇa, "mīyante jñāyante iti māyāḥ karmāṇi," i.e. "māyāḥ" (nom. pl.) means ritual practices because they "are known" (from √mā, to know). In R.V. x. 53.9 too Sāyaṇa takes the word to mean "karma." We are inclined to say that this derivation of Sāyaṇa is a little far-fetched. Another rather fanciful derivation—giving the meaning correctly none the less—is "māyā = mā yā, i.e., that which is not—that which truly is not but still appears to be." This is, however, a merely interesting derivation without any principles of etymology.

Another way to derive it would be "māti (svātmānam) darśayati iti māyā," i.e., "that which shows itself—that which appears to our view (without having any real existence)." This will be from √mā, to show.

Hence, the conception of māyā as the causal will-power (icchā-śakti or prajñā) may be derived from √mā, to know; and, as the effectual state of the world as illusion, from √mā, to measure, to build, etc.

To sum up: we have seen that the word "māyā" meant in R.V.—

(1) Supernatural power, mysterious will-power, wonderful skill, and that the idea of the

underlying mystery being more emphasized later on, it came to mean in A.V.

(2) Magic, illusion. And, further, we saw that in the Brāhmaṇas and the Upaniṣads also it meant

(3) illusion, and that this meaning was more and more fixed subsequently, till in the time of Śaṅkara it was established beyond doubt. The sense of "illusion" may easily be found to exist in form even in the Vedic usage of the term, e.g., where in the R.V. it meant "power or skill" it always meant "supernatural" or "wondrous" power and not the ordinary physical power.

The idea of *mystery* or "wonder" always was present, and it is this very element that in its developed form gives the sense of "illusion" or "appearance." The idea of "magic" in A.V. formed a link between the old meaning of "supernatural power" and the modern one of "appearance" or "illusion." As we have already pointed out, "māyā" has been viewed principally from two aspects—

(1) As the *principle* of creation—māyā as a *cause*—corresponding to the sense of śakti (wondrous power), or

(2) As the phenomenal creation itself—māyā as an *effect*—corresponding to the sense of "illusion," "appearance," etc.

This short summary, we hope, will suffice as an

introduction to the conception of māyā in the following chapter. The meaning of the term having been discussed, we will now attempt to trace the development of the theory or the idea of Māyā from the Vedic times down to Śaṅkara's, when its usage was finally settled, limiting ourselves to the system of the Vedānta proper.

If we were to attempt to trace the conception of Māyā or its alternative conceptions in other systems, it would lead us out of our present scope. We hope, however, to be able sometime in the near future to write a separate treatise on this doctrine with special reference to its place in modern Hindu philosophy and its analogies in other Eastern and Western Religions and Philosophies. For the present we have to confine ourselves mainly to the historical view of the conception of Māyā within the system of the Vedānta.

DEVELOPMENT OF THE CONCEPTION OF MĀYĀ

CHAPTER II

DEVELOPMENT OF THE CONCEPTION OF MĀYĀ.

AFTER a brief philological survey of the *word* māyā, we now turn to the *idea* itself. The word and the idea are not to be confused; since such a confusion is productive of various false assumptions as to the doctrine of māyā in relation to its place in Indian thought. There are not a few who boldly allege that the doctrine is distinctively of a late origin and growth, an after-thought or a subsequent suggestion of some of the later Vedāntins of the purely Idealistic temperament. The idea of Māyā, they pretend, is wholly wanting in the earlier philosophical treatises of the Hindus, viz., the Upaniṣads, etc. Without anticipating any discussion on this point, we may only state that such thinkers seem to us to be entirely mistaken. Hence our main thesis in this chapter will be to show, with the aid of suitable authoritative quotations from our philosophic literature, that the *idea* of Māyā is very old—certainly older than the *word* māyā. The *word* in its usual sense, of course, occurs for the first time in the Śvetāśvatara Upaniṣad (iv. 10), but the *idea* may be traced to the later stage of the Vedic civilization. We shall endeavour to show that the conception, though not in a systematic and organic form, is already found in the R.V. and the Upaniṣads.

Philosophy, as reflective thought, or the thinking consideration of things,[1] did actually begin with *things*; that is to say, the first germs of philosophy began to appear with an attempt to explain the concrete realities in the environment, i.e., the Universe. A yearning was noticeable in the human breast to comprehend the source of all existence. And as all higher development is from the concrete to the abstract, thought too followed the same course, and after passing through the stages in which the different forces of nature, or various other elements, such as water, air, fire, etc., began to be imagined as the chief source of all existences, the point was reached where the "many" was found to yield no satisfactory explanation of its being, and a desire was felt to know the mystery, the underlying unity. With the advance in thought, the principle of unity attracted more and more attention, so much so that as early as in R.V. i. 164 ("ekaṃ sad viprā bahudhā vadanti"—i.e., the poets speak of the One Being under various names), the multiplicity was felt to be due to a mode of *speech* only, not real in itself,

[1] Cf. Schwegler, *Geschichte der Philosophie*, Stuttgart, Einleitung: "Philosophieren ist Nachdenken, denkende Betrachtung der Dinge."

only the One having real existence. The innumerable Vedic gods began thus to be conceived as not at war with one another, but only manifestations of One God. Monotheism conquered Polytheism in its exclusive sense. The last book of the R.V. is particularly rich in philosophic hymns, many of which strike a chord of the same sentiment of " unity underlying diversity." The bold speculation of the ancient Vedic people is picturesquely portrayed in R.V. x. 129—one of the earliest records known of an attempt at explaining the cosmogonic mystery by grasping the idea of unity. It is one of the most sublime and exalted hymns in the R.V., both from the philosophic and the literary standpoints, and is a true index to the early mystic thought of the Hindus. To a somewhat prejudiced mind it may appear as a mere conglomeration of contradictions and a piece of abstract sophistry. But it is one of the finest songs that any literature may be proud of. Deussen describes it as " the most remarkable monument of the oldest philosophy,[1] " and has translated it into German.[2] As the hymn is very important for our purpose, we give our own translation as follows—

---

[1] Deussen, *Outlines of Indian Philosophy*, Berlin, 1907, p. 13, l. 20.

[2] Deussen, *Geschichte der Philosophie*, vol. i., p. 126, and also in his *Geheimlehre des Veda*, zweite Auflage, Leipzig, 1907, p. 3. The hymn has been translated by many, but most of the translations seem to be incorrect in places.

R.V. x. 129.

1. Then was neither Being nor Non-Being,
   No realm of air, no sky beyond;
   What enveloped all? Where? In whose care?
   Were waters there, the deep abyss?

2. 'Twas neither death nor life immortal,
   No night was there, no day's appearance;
   The One in its spontaneity did airless breathe,
   Beyond it naught was in existence.

3. Darkness was there; at first by darkness covered,
   The world was ocean without distinction;
   But a pregnant germ lay hidden in shell,
   The One engendered by force of heat.

4. Within it at first arose Desire,
   Which was the primal seed of mind;
   The root of Being in Non-Being Sages
   Searching by wisdom in the heart discovered.

5. When like a ray their being they spread,
   What was below? what was above?
   Seed-bearers were there, great powers too,
   Spontaneity beneath and effort above.

6. Who knows, in sooth? Who here can tell?
   Whence it became? Whence this creation?
   The gods came later than its creation,
   So who can tell whence all this arose?

7. From whom arose this whole creation,
   Whether he produced it or not he;
   Who in highest heaven surveys it,
   He knows it well—or even not he.

This marks the beginnings of philosophical thought in India. The same conception of the basal unity of the world afterwards gave rise to Greek philosophy in the Eleatic monism. Xenophanes started his polemic against the anthropomorphism in popular Greek religion and was the first among Greek thinkers to declare "All is one." A little later Parmenides too developed, as his chief principle, the same idea of the essential oneness of being and thought. We point out this fact simply to show that it was quite natural and legitimate that the Vedic poets should begin their philosophical speculation with their yearning to comprehend the underlying *unity* of the world. That the yearning was natural is amply shown by almost exactly the same tendencies being found in other philosophies, especially in that of Greece. As in Greece, so in India, philosophy was born as "the child of wonder."

Garbe, who has done a good deal of useful work in the Sāṅkhya, has unfortunately failed to realize the spirit in which the above hymn was composed by the Vedic Aryans, and finds in it as well as in other philosophical hymns in the R.V., "unclear and self-contradictory trains of thought."[1] We fail to perceive any such contradictions. The various explanations are in themselves demanded by the very mysterious nature of the problem. It may be remarked in passing that the Being and Non-Being

[1] Richard Garbe, *The Philosophy of Ancient India*, Chicago, 1897, p. 1.

spoken of in the hymn do not stand in antithesis (as they do in early Greek philosophy); on the contrary, they are *one*, though they are *two* from *our* way of looking at them.[1] The undeveloped state, known as *kāraṇāvasthā*, is spoken of as *Non-Being*—it does *not* mean the *negation of Being*; while the manifested state is called by the name of *Being*.

This also explains why Being is said to be born of Non-Being in R.V. x. 72. 2–3, and the root of the former is discovered in the latter (R.V. x. 129. 4). There might appear many such contradictions implied in the use of terms, but they are only *seeming* contradictions, and vanish as soon as the real reconciliation (vyavasthā) is made out.

Now, after attaining a *consciousness* of the *oneness* of all things, the next step was naturally a quest after the nature of this unity. An attempt is made to determine it in R.V. x. 121, where, after describing the majesty and wonder of the vast network of creation, the poet at last names Prajāpati as the unknown god, the ultimate unity of all creation.

> "Prajāpati, than thou there is no other,
> Who holds in his embrace the whole creation."

This idea of Prajāpati is subsequently transformed under the name of Brahman or Ātman in the Upani-

[1] On this idea see Śaṅkara's commentary on Vedānta-Sūtras, i. 4. 15, p. 376, ll. 7–10 (Bibl. Ind. edn.).

ṣads. However, in another Vedic hymn (R.V. x. 90) we see the same power attributed to "*Puruṣa*" (who, we believe, is one with Prajāpati in general conception), and in R.V. x. 81 and 82 to Viśvakarman. In R.V. x. 72 the same functions are referred to Brahmaṇaspati—

"Brahmaṇaspati like a smith
Together forged this universe;
When gods existed not as yet,
Then Being from Non-Being did arise."

Later on, Prajāpati is identified with the creating word [1] (the Greek "Logos") in R.V. x. 125, and with "the sacrifice and the year" as principles of

[1] On the relation between the Indian conception of *Vāc* and the Greek conception of λόγος, see Weber's *Indische Studien*, vol. ix. Cf. also Max Heinze, *Die Lehre vom Logos in der Griechischen Philosophie*, Oldenberg, 1872. In numerous passages *Vāc* also appears as the consort of Prajāpati, the creator.

R.V. x. 90, has been translated by Max Müller, *Ancient Sk. Lit.* (1859), p. 569; Muir, O.S.T., iv. 16; Ludwig, No. 948; Grassmann, ii. 398; Max Müller, *Hibbert Lectures* (1882), p. 301; Henry W. Wallis, *Cosmology of the R.V.*, p. 50; Max Müller, *Vedic Hymns*, S.B.E., xxxii. 1; Deussen, *Geschichte*, i. 1. 132.

With some variants, this hymn is found in A.V. iv. 2, which has been translated by Weber, xviii. 8; Oldenberg, *Die Hymnen des R.V.*, i. 314 f., Bloomfield, JAOS, xv. 184. V.S. xxxi. 18 (=Śvetāś. Up. iii. 8: Muir v. p. 373) refer to Puruṣa:—

"I know this great Purusha, resplendent as the sun, above the darkness. It is by knowing him that a man the world, R.V. x. 190. We here insert the former in our own translation, as it is one of the typical hymns of the Rigvedic speculation and is important for our purpose—

R.V. x. 125.[1]

Vāc.

1. I wander with the Rudras and the Vasus,
With the Ādityas and the Viśve Devās ;
I support both, Mitra and Varuṇa,
Indra and Agni, and the Aśvins two.

2. I support Soma, swelling with juice,
I support Tvaṣṭṛ, Pūṣan and Bhaga ;
'Tis I who give wealth to the zealous offerer,
To the sacrificer who presses Soma.

3. I am the queen, the showerer of riches,
The knowing, first of the worshipped ones ;
Me have the gods in many forms displayed,
Me, living everywhere and entering all things.

ever passes death. There is no other road to go." Cf. V.S. xxxii. 2.

Muir, p. 374. All winkings of the eye have sprung from Puruṣa, the resplendent. No one has limited him either above, or below, or in the middle.

The first two verses of R.V. x. 90 are given in the Śvetāś-vat. Up. iii. 14, 15. Cf. A.V. xix. 4, 5. 6. 7. Colebrooke's *Misc. Essays*, i. 167 and note in p. 309.

[1] For translations of the hymn, see Colebrooke, *Asiatic Researches*, vol. viii., Calcutta, 1805, or *Miscellaneous Essays*, i., p. 28 ; Weber's article on "Vāc and Logos," *Ind. Stud.*, ix. (1865), 473 ; Deussen, *Geschichte*, vol. i. 1. 146 f. ; Griffith, i. 171 ; Weber, xviii. 117. The whole hymn is found with slight variants in A.V. iv. 30.

4. Through me he eats food, who sees,
Who breathes, who hears what's spoken ;
Not knowing me they stay by me,
Hear thou of fame, I tell thee what's not easy to know.
worthy of belief.
(*Muir.*)
to be credited.
(*Whitney.*)

5. It is I myself who declare this truth,
Agreeable to gods and men alike ;
I make him powerful, whom I love,
Him a Brahmā (Brāhmaṇa), a Ṛṣi, a sage.

6. It's I who bend the bow for Rudra,
That his arrow may strike the foe of Brāhmaṇa,
It's I who fight for my peoples' sake,
It's I who have entered both heaven and earth.

7. I create Father (Dyaus), first on the world's summit, [1]
My birth-place is in the waters, in the ocean ;
Then I into all things existing enter,
And touch yonder heaven with my body.

8. It's I who blow forth like the wind,
Spreading into being all that exist ;
Beyond the sky, beyond this earth,
So great have I by my glory become.

The unity of existence could not be more simply and emphatically pronounced than in these hymns. When the goddess *Vāc* says in stanza 3,

---

[1] This line is difficult to translate quite accurately. The extant translations do not throw any light on it. Whitney too leaves it open to doubt in his *Atharva-veda, Trans. and Notes*, vol. i., p. 201.

> "Me have the gods in many forms displayed,
> Me, living everywhere and entering all things,"

she repeats the same thought we have already referred to, which again is expressed by the Ṛṣi *Dīrghatamas* while praising Agni—

> "Of the one existence, the sages speak in diverse ways."—
> R.V. i. 164.

And the same thought was later on brought out by Yāska (who lived about the fifth century, B.C.) :—"The One Ātman is sung in many ways" (Nir. vii. 5, Roth's ed., p. 11). Some of the other Vedic hymns in which this conception of the underlying unity of being is brought out are R.V. x. 81, 82, 90, 121, etc., which we can only refer to, instead of translating here. All this clearly shows that this idea of unity is as old as the Vedic civilization, that the ancient Indian Ṛṣīs were quite aware of the oneness of being and gave a poetic expression to the same thought in many beautiful strains.

It is needless to multiply instances from the other three Vedas, since the R.V. is the chief source of these and is in itself the oldest and most important one. Most of the hymns of the other Vedas are bodily transferred from the R.V. and arranged in different ways to meet the spirit and requirements of each. We may, however, note in passing that the same idea of the unity of being is discovered in the following stanzas from the A.V.—

"Aditi is heaven, Aditi atmosphere,
Aditi mother, she father, she son;
All the gods are Aditi, the five races,
Aditi is what is born, Aditi what is to be born."
A.V. vii. 6. 1.[1]

"Whoever know the Brahman in man, they know the most exalted one; whoever know the most exalted one, and whoever know Prajāpati, whoever know the chief Brāhmaṇa, they know also accordingly the Skambha."

"The great being (Yakṣa) [2] is absorbed in austere fervour in the midst of the world, on the surface of the waters. In it are set whatever gods there are, as the branches of a tree around the trunk." [3]

A.V. x. 7. 17, and 38.

"What moves, flies and stands, breathing,
not-breathing and winking; that
universal form sustains the earth,
that combined becomes One only."
A.V. x. 8. 11.

"Prajāpati goes about within the womb;
Unseen, yet is manifestly born." [4]
A.V. x. 8. 13.

---

[1] Compare R.V. i. 89. 10; V.S. xxv. 23; T.A. i. 13. 2; and M.S. iv. 14. 4. For a similar sentiment in reference to Virāj, see A.V. ix. 10. 24.

[2] For a discussion on "Yakṣa" (cf. also A.V. x. 8. 15) see Geldner, *Vedische Studien*, iii. 126 ff.; also *Kena Up.*, iii. 14–25; Deussen, *Sechzig Upaniṣads*, p. 204, Einleitung.

[3] This is from the well-known A.V. hymn on the Skambha or the Frame of Creation. For translation see Muir's *Sanskrit Texts*, vol. v., pp. 380–384; Ludwig, p. 400; Deussen, *Geschichte*, i. l. 310; Griffith, ii. 26; and Whitney's A.V. vol. ii. p. 589. The translation is taken from Whitney.

[4] For translation of A.V. x. 8. see Muir, v., p. 386;

"Knowing the soul, free from desire, wise, immortal, self-existent, satisfied with the essence, not deficient in any respect, one is not afraid of death." [1]

A.V. x. 8. 44.

"They call him Indra, Mitra, Varuṇa, Agni; likewise he is the heavenly-winged eagle; what is one the sages name variously; they call him Agni, Yama, Mātariśvan." [2]

A.V. ix. 10. 28.

These typical passages point to a continuation of the same idea in the A.V. The Brāhmaṇas, the exegetical treatises on the Samhitāś, being mainly guided by the Śruti,[3] and starting with the object of making explicit what is implicitly implied in the mantras, may naturally be supposed not to swerve from the general spirit of the latter. What is already explicit in the mantras is sometimes only *emphasized* in these treatises. The transition from the earlier thought of the Samhitā to that of the Brāhmaṇas may be noticed, for instance, in R.V. x. 81, where the question is asked—

Ludwig, p. 395; Deussen, *Geschichte*, i. l. 318; Griffith, ii. 34.

[1] Compare what Deussen remarks on this passage: "die erste und älteste Stelle, die wir kennen, in der ruckhaltlos der Ātman als Weltprincip proklamiert wird, A.V. x. 8. 44," (*Geschichte der Philosophie*, vol. i., p. 334).

[2] See Whitney's A.V., p. 561.

[3] The Brāhmaṇas in regard to their subject-matter are supposed by some to be "uditānuvādāḥ"—i.e., they explain in detail what is already given in the Veda. (Cf. Yāska, *Nirukta*, i. 16. Roth's ed., p. 37, "uditānuvādaḥ sa bhavati.")

"Which was the tree, which was the wood, of which they hewed the earth and heaven?"

This question is repeated in the text of the Taittirīya Brāhmaṇa, and is followed by the answer—

"Brahman was the tree, the wood from which they hewed the earth and heaven."

The conception of Prajāpati and of Puruṣa is also developed in the Vājasaneyī Samhitā and the Taittirīya Brāhmaṇa.[1] The simple note of unity is also sounded, for instance, in the Śatap. Br., iv. 2. 2. 1.—

"sarvaṃ hy ayam ātmā," i.e., "this soul is everything."

We are, however, mainly concerned with the *Upaniṣads*, which are, as a rule, the final positions of the Brāhmaṇas. The word is derived from the root *sad*, to sit, with the prepositions *upa*, near, and *ni*=very (adverbial), and conveys the sense, "that which is imparted to a pupil when he sits very near his teacher"—hence, "secret doctrine." The Upaniṣads may, therefore, be said to embody the esoteric doctrines of the Vedas. They mostly contain philosophical expositions, elucidations and discussions on some Vedic passages, and by themselves form a more or less complete and comprehensive philoso-

[1] Cf. V.S. viii. 36; xxxi. 18–21; xxxiv. 1–6, etc.; T.A. i. 23. 9; T.B. ii. 8. 8. 8–10; ii. 8. 9. 6–7; iii. 12. 9.

phical system, which is the kernel of the whole of the later philosophy. Their idealism is the groundstone of the later Vedānta. They are canonical, and quotations from them are held by tradition ever complete and self-sufficient and require no further support. They are final authorities.[1] The general trend of their thought is towards a thorough-going monism, which in its germinal form existed even in the Vedas, as we have shown above. Their fundamental formula may be expressed in a well-known distich—

> " Brahma satyaṃ jagan mithyā
> Jīvo brahmaiva nāparaḥ."

i. e.,

> " Brahman is the Reality, the universe is false,
> The Ātman is Brahman, nothing else."

In other words, there is only *one* Reality, call it Brahman or Ātman—what you will, and the world around us which appears so real is not so. This is the central thought which has been so admirably

[1] It may be interesting to know that the Upaniṣads form the chief source of quotations in Śaṅkara's Śārīraka-Bhāṣya. According to the frequency of their occurrence in Śaṅkara's monumental commentary they may thus be arranged in order—

Chāndogya, 809 quotations ; Bṛhadāraṇyaka, 565 ; Taittirīya, 142 ; Muṇḍaka, 129 ; Kaṭha, 103 ; Kauṣītaki, 88 ; Śvetāśvatara, 53 ; Agni-Rahasya (Śat. Br. x.), 40 ; Praśṇa, 38 ; Aitareya (Ait. Ār. ii. 4–6), 22 ; Jābāla, 13 ; Nārāyaṇīya (Taitt. Ār. x.), 9 ; Īśa (Vāj. Sam. xl.), 8 ; Paiṅgī, 6 ; Kena, 5.

expanded and developed in various ways in the Upaniṣads, and what we call the doctrine of Māyā is nothing more than an attempt to explain this fact in detail, to show how it is impossible for the world to be anything more than an " appearance " as distinguished from " Reality," which strictly speaking is only Brahman.

We now come to one of the most important parts of our present subject, viz., the development of the theory of Māyā through the Upaniṣads down to Śaṅkara. We may remark at the outset that the theory may be enunciated in two ways: (1) That the world is an illusion or appearance, and (2) That the only reality is the Ātman. These two statements mean the same thing, so that the passages which emphasize the statement that the Ātman is the only reality mean most transparently that all else (i.e., other than the Ātman, viz., the world, etc.) is not real.

The Upaniṣads when read through without any guiding principle seem to bristle with startling contradictions. The world is described as pervaded by the Ātman, and it is said that all this is Brahman, while at the same time it is asserted that the world is unreal; again, it is declared that the Ātman created the world, while yet it is true that there is no world besides Brahman. All such and other statements would perhaps baffle all attempts at explanation if only we looked at the external aspect, and some readers of the Upaniṣads may consequently with great impatience pronounce these books to be nothing but a mass of crude contradictions. But it is not so. There is to be traced within the Upaniṣads a certain development (" degeneration," from another point of view) of Pure Idealism. In the Bṛh. Upaniṣad[1] are found certain passages, chiefly in the first four chapters, which are connected with the discourse of Yājñavalkya, and which furnish the oldest idealistic conception as far as we know.

Yājñavalkya's standpoint is purely metaphysical. He was the leader of the sages, and he is said to have quite realized his identity with the Brahman.

One seems to be carried away by the simple force of his lofty utterances, which appear to be poured out from the very depths of his heart after a thorough realization of the truths they contain. His dialogues with his wife Maitreyī and with the king Janaka appeal to us as the clearest enunciations of the true standpoint of Idealism, which on account of its extremely monistic conception cannot be surpassed, a more thorough-going monism being *prima facie* impossible. The burden of the whole throughout is that

" the Ātman is the only reality,"

which at once implies that the world is not real. We

[1] The Bṛhad Up. and the Chān. Up. seem to be the oldest among the collection. It is rather difficult to say which of these two is the older. Judging from style and other evidences, especially the parallel texts, etc., it appears that the Brh. was the older.

shall now examine some of these passages, in order to give a more concrete idea of the general position maintained by the old idealist—

> " Ātmā vā are draṣṭavyaḥ śrotavyo mantavyo nididhyāsitavyo Maitreyi—Ātmano vā are darśanena śravaṇena matyā vijñānenaidaṃ sarvam viditam " (Bṛh. Up. ii. 4. 5).
> i.e.,
> The Ātman is to be seen, heard, understood, meditated—O Maitreyī ; by seeing, hearing, understanding and realizing the Ātman, all this world is known.

This is repeated again in iv. 5. 6.

The same idea is expressed by means of three similes, viz., of the drum (dundubhiḥ), the conch-shell, and the lyre. As by holding fast the drum, the conch-shell, the lyre, when they are being beaten, all their sounds are as it were caught together, so by knowing the Ātman all is known, i.e., all worth knowing becomes already known. When these instruments are being sounded one cannot hear anything else and is confused in the multiplicity of the sounds, but on taking possession of the instruments—the source of all the sounds—one seems to have mastered the discord and to have found the key to it all. So is the Ātman the key to the all, viz., to the universe ; when the Ātman is known then there is nothing else that is worth knowing ; the multiplicity perishes and the unity asserts its sway. The following is the passage containing these three similes—

> " sa yathā dundubher hanyamānasya na bāhyān śabdān

śaknuyād grahaṇāya, dundubhes tu grahaṇena dundubhyāghātasya vā śabdo gṛhītaḥ."—Bṛh. Up. ii. 4. 7.[1]

i.e.,

As in the midst of drum-beating one is unable to grasp the outer sounds, but on grasping the drum itself the sound produced by the drum-beating is also grasped.

A most remarkable passage, which in the clearest phraseology endorses the conception of Māyā, is found in Bṛh. ii. 4. 14. It runs thus—

"Yatra hi dvaitam iva bhavati tad itara itaraṃ jighrati tad itara itaram paśyati tad itara itaraṃ śṛṇoti tad itara itaram abhivadati tad itara itaram manute tad itara itaraṃ vijānāti, yatra vā asya sarvam ātmaivābhūt tat kena kaṃ jighret tat kena kam paśyet tat kena kaṃ śṛṇuyāt tat kena kam abhivadet tat kena kam manvīta tat kena kaṃ vijānīyād yenedam sarvaṃ vijānāti tam kena vijānīyād vijñātāram are kena vijānīyād iti."

Bṛh. Up. ii. 4. 14.[2]

(*Trans.*)—

For where there is duality, *as it were*, there sees another another thing, there smells another another thing, there hears another another thing, there speaks another of another thing, there thinks another of another thing, there knows another another thing; but where all has become nothing but the Ātman, there how can one smell anything, how see anything, how hear anything, how speak of anything, how think of anything, how know anything. By what shall one know *him*, by whom knows one this all? By what shall one know the knower?

---

[1] Cf. also Ibid., ii. 4. 8. The same passage is again found in iv. 5. 8–10.

[2] This famous passage reappears in Bṛh. Up. iv. 5. 15, with slight alterations.

The word *iva* (= as it were) is important here. " Where there is duality, as it were " shows that duality, which refers to the multiplicity (nānātva) in the world, is unreal ; in other words, it is only an appearance. The conception of subject and object is only possible when each of them has at least a distinguishable existence. But when all this " otherness " is found to be false, that which was called the " object " disappears and only the one Ātman remains as the knower. In that sense even the word " subject " (in the current sense) would be inadmissible, since it is only a relative term, and when the object perishes, the idea of the subject also goes with it. The distinction is lost, that which was real remains as the one, and the unreal, which never did actually exist, is found to be a nullity. The Ātman being itself the Knower, the self-luminous, the Universal Spirit, does not require any medium to be known. That is the idea which Yājñavalkya so simply and yet so forcibly conveys when he says—

" vijñātāram are kena vijānīyāt ? "

i.e.,

By what shall the knower be known ?

Further on Yājñavalkya, while instructing the sage Uṣasta on the nature of the Ātman, says—

" na dṛṣter draṣṭāram paśyer na śruter śrotāraṃ śṛṇuyān na mater mantāram manvīthā na vijñāter vijñātaraṃ vijānīyāḥ eṣa ta ātmā sarvāntaro 'to 'nyad ārttam."

Bṛh. Up. iii. 4. 2.

(*Trans.*)—

" Thou couldst not see the seer of sight, thou couldst

not hear the hearer of hearing, thou couldst not think the thinker of thought, thou couldst not know the knower of knowing. This thy Ātman is within every being, all else is full of sorrow (*ārtta*).

Here it is shown how the Ātman is so near within one's self that one does not need to go a long way to search for it. If the idea of distance is to be used at all (which is really inadmissible) it may be said to be the *nearest*. Those who go out to seek it anywhere else by external means never find it. The attempts at a rigid definition of Brahman are all futile. This thought is like that of the popular tale so well known in India. A man had his little child on his shoulder and was strolling about in the street. All of a sudden, forgetting that he had the child with him, he began to proclaim in a loud voice throughout the city: "I have lost my child; who has seen it, kindly let me know." At last a passer-by, observing his gross error, gave him a smart slap in the face and turned his eyes upward, when to his utter surprise he found that the "lost child" was still on him.[1] So exactly is the Ātman always in us. In fact we are never justified in saying "in us" as truly speaking "it *is* ourself," not "it is *in* us"; the latter would imply that we are different from the Ātman. The sage here declares, therefore, that this Ātman is the subject of

[1] The proverb is technically known in Punjābī as "kuc-chaḍ kuḍi śahara ḍhanḍorā."

all knowledge, hence unknowable. The categories of all knowledge break down when stretched with a view to their application to the Ātman. And as to all else, which is "the other," the sage says "ato anyat ārtam," i.e., all else is full of sorrow. This phrase is repeated again in iii. 5. 1, in a dialogue with Kahola. This "other than the Self," i.e., the so-called world, is again denied its reality in iii. 8. 11, where Yājñavalkya is instructing Gārgī (who was of a highly philosophic temperament) in the mysterious love of the Brahman.

In Bṛh. Up. iv. 4. 4, again, the simile of a goldsmith is employed. As he by taking a bit of gold moulds it into various newer and more beautiful forms, so the Ātman is supposed to create through *Avidyā* various forms, such as the Pitṛis, the Gandharvas, the gods, Prajāpati, Brahmā, etc. Here all the variety of forms is spoken of as *avidyā*, hence unreal. It may, however, be pointed out that similes illustrate only a special aspect of truth and should not be carried beyond their legitimate sphere.

The phrase "avidyām gamayitvā" occurs in this mantra as well as in the preceding one, where an example of the caterpillar is given.

Another remarkable passage that lends a decisive support to this pure idealism occurs in Bṛh. iv. 4. 19—

> "manasaiva anudraṣṭavyam
> neha nānā 'sti kiñcana,
> mṛtyoḥ sa mṛtyum āpnoti
> ya iha nāneva paśyati."

(*Trans.*)—

It is to be perceived by the mind alone,
there is here no multiplicity whatever;
who sees here as it were "many"
passes from death to death.

That multiplicity, the characteristic of the universe, is false is the high-sounding note here, and it is still further emphasized by saying that he who sees *as it were* a plurality actually existing is never saved, but is over and over subject to the pangs of birth and death in this *saṃsāra*. The conception of Māyā exhibits itself in such passages clearly, and yet many do not see it. Here also attention may specially be drawn to the word *iva*—"as it were"—which implies that the multiplicity is only an *appearance*, an "as it were." Truly speaking, this "as it were" should be supplied in almost all passages where the Upaniṣads speak of "the other." It would be quite in keeping with the spirit of true idealism.

This exactly is the highest (and the truest) standpoint of the Upaniṣads. When they deny in such clear and distinct terms the existence of "the many," it means that they refuse to concede any reality to the world from that standpoint, the idea of the world being meaningless without all this *nānā* (multiplicity). Abstract "the many" and you bring the world to a zero-point, nothing remains behind; all vanishes.

All the words which we use in our every-day

life to express the various distinctions among objects, or "the many," are mere abuses of our speech, since they are ill-spent or wasted, "the many" having no existence at all. Only "the One" exists, and when that is known all else is known, and the use of words breaks down. This idea is expressed in Bṛh. iv. 4. 21—

> "tam eva dhīro vijñāya prajñām kurvīta brāhmaṇaḥ,
> nānudhyāyād bahūn śabdān vāco viglāpanaṃ hi tat."
> (*Trans.*)—
> Knowing him alone let the wise Brāhmaṇa form his prajñā (understanding), let him not meditate on many words, for that is simply the fatigue of *vāc* (speech).

This in brief is the spirit of Yājñavalkya's Idealism. It may conveniently be viewed in three aspects :—

1. *The Ātman is the only reality.*
2. *The Ātman is the subject of knowledge in us* (cf. iii. 4. 2, iii. 7. 23, iii. 8. 11), hence
3. *The Ātman is itself unknowable.* (Cf. ii. 4. 14, iv. 5. 15, etc.)

It may be pointed out that there is no contradiction, as many have been led to suppose, in the statements "the Ātman is unknowable" and "by knowing the Ātman all is known" or "the Ātman alone is to be known." The word "knowledge" is used in two different aspects. The Ātman is "*unknowable*" when by knowledge is meant a synthesis of the subject and object, or when it is supposed that speech is able to describe the Self. The knower, the self, can know the known or the objects, but how can the knower be known? The truth of the idea is not very difficult to grasp, if one just reflects seriously for a moment. If all things are known only through the "I," by what can the "I" itself be known? The fact of this self-consciousness is ultimate in itself.[1] Hence in this sense the knower cannot be known, while at the same time no knowledge could be more sure than that of the knower, the self. Here "knowledge" is used in a higher and different sense, viz., self-realization or experience (*anubhava*). Even the greatest sceptic could not reasonably deny the existence of the "I," and a higher knowledge of this self means the realization of the falsity of the not-self and of the oneness of the Ātman. The seeming paradox therefore disappears on a little deeper understanding.

Now this oldest, simplest and most thoroughgoing idealism is found chiefly in the Bṛh. Up., as shown above, but it is not totally ousted by the later doctrines in revolt, and so appears scattered here and there among the others in the chief Upaniṣads as well. The doctrine of the sole reality of

[1] Similar analogies may be noticed in European philosophy. Descartes, e.g., started with this very fact, *Cogito, ergo sum*. Almost all idealists start with self-consciousness as the ultimate fact.

the Ātman—hence of the falsity of the world, "the Many"—has never been totally given up later on. Certainly it has been gradually obscured—though at the same time shining through by its inherent light—by the huge mass of more realistic or anti-idealistic notions. Such conceptions we may have occasion to refer to briefly later on. We hasten now to show how this supreme monistic conception runs through the other Upaniṣads like a string through the beads of a garland.

Turning to the Chāndogya Up., we at once meet with the famous dialogue between Aruṇi and his son, Śvetaketu. The son having studied all the Vedas, etc., for twelve years with his teacher, returned to his father a swollen-headed young scholar. The father tested his knowledge by asking him if he knew anything about *that* by which all that is unheard becomes heard and the unknown becomes the known, etc. The son, failing to answer, requests his father to explain to him that knowledge, and the sage Aruṇi teaches Śvetaketu by the following concrete examples—

> "yāthā somya ekena mṛtpiṇḍena sarvam mṛṇmayaṃ vijñātam syād vācārambhaṇaṃ vikāro nāmadheyam mṛttikety eva satyam.
>
> Chān. Up. vi. 1. 4.[1]

---

[1] Cf. the same idea in different similes in the following two mantras, Chān. Up. vi. 1. 5–6.

(*Trans.*)—

As, O good one, by (the knowledge of) one ball of earth everything of the nature of earth is known; the change (or modification) is an extension of words, a mere name, only the earth is true.[1]

Here it is said that by knowing the one the all is known. As all the forms into which clay is

[1] Some critics of the Vedānta discover in this passage a corroboration of the theory of *Pariṇāmavāda*. They contend that as the various things of earth (jar, pot, etc.) are transformations of the earth, not being creations of the imagination (*Sat* coming out of *Sat* only), so is the world as *sat* a development of a subtle *sat*. Some of the modern evolutionists would also urge that the world is simply a process of evolution of the one principle—by whatever name you may call it, *matter, spirit, thought*, or the Ātman. According to these views the Self transforms itself into *Natura Naturata*, and as a *real* cause has a *real* effect, the world must be a reality. The Sāṅkhya system is also based on such a theory, which makes the world a reality, being an actual modification or development of *real matter*.

This view appears to be based on an exclusively one-sided interpretation of the passage. The whole rests on the assumption that things like the jar, etc., are actual transformations of earth. But the passage seems to us to endorse the purely idealistic standpoint, making the world, to use later phraseology, a *vivarta* instead of a *vikāra*.

The *vivarta* of a substance is simply its appearance, which in no way implies any alteration in the thing itself; while a *vikāra* is the transformation of the substance itself. (" Vivarta = atattvato 'nyathā prathā; vikāra = satattvato 'nyathā prathā." To take a well-known technical example, milk is substantially transformed into curd or junket: these are two wholly different states—one cannot discover any *milk* when it is changed into *curd*. But a jar of earth, even after individuating itself as a *jar*, does moulded are known by knowing clay, so the manifold world is known by knowing the one Ātman, since all reality is the Ātman and the non-Ātman does not really exist. The "many forms" are merely "the beginning of speech" (vācārambhaṇam), only a mere name (nāmadheyam) without reality. The plurality is all a mere *name*, hence unreal.[1]

In Ch. vi. 2. 1–2, where the process of creation is described from the empirical standpoint, the words "ekam-eva-advitiyam" ("the only one without a second") occur, which point out the essential oneness of the Ātman.

Again, in Chān. Up. vii. 23. 1 we read—

> "yo vai bhūmā tat sukham, nālpe sukham asti bhūmaiva sukham bhūmā tv eva vijijñāsitavya iti."
>
> (*Trans.*)—
>
> That which is the Bhūmā (the Great) is happiness, there

---

not cease to be earth; it is earth inside and out, the idea of *jar* is simply due to the limitations of name and form, which are decidedly mind-dependent. The evidence of the jar *quâ* jar is not at all independent. So also when a rope is mistaken for a snake, it is not *transformed* into the latter. It is the mind imposing the conception of the *snake* on the *rope*. The former has no independent existence. This example of the rope, etc., is a typical one for the vivarta-theory, but it is evident how the implications of the analogy of the earth correspond with those of this one. Hence the passage, judged both from its contextual spirit and analogies, supports the idea of *vivarta*, not of *vikāra*.

[1] The words "vācārambhanaṃ vikāro nāmadheyam" again occur in Chān. Up. vi, 4. 1–3.

is no happiness in the small. Only the Bhūmā is happiness. The Bhūmā is therefore to be searched after.

In this passage Brahman is spoken of as Bhūmā (the Great), and only He is said to be *bliss*; all that is not Brahman (= the Ātman) is *alpam* (little) and misery. Only that Bhūmā is worthy of being known. The words *tu eva* are important, since they emphasize the exclusive knowledge of the Ātman alone. In the following khaṇḍa (Chān. vii. 24. 1) that Bhūmā is defined as—

" yatra na anyat paśyati na anyat śṛṇoti na anyat vijānāti sa bhūmā."

(*Trans.*)—

Where none other sees, none other hears, none other knows, that is Bhūmā.

And the Alpa is defined as—

" yatra anyat paśyati anyat śṛṇoti anyad vijānāti tad alpam."

(*Trans.*)—

Where another sees, another hears, another knows, that is Alpa.

The latter is declared to be perishable (" tat martyam "). When the nature of multiplicity is realized to be false " the other " (anya) will cease to exist and only the Bhūmā will shine in his everlasting luminosity.

The Taitt. Up. does not contain much on the subject. It is mainly concerned with the more realistic conception of the creation of the world from the Ātman.[1] There is of course a famous passage on the unknowableness of the Ātman.

> " yato vāco nivartante aprāpya manasā saha,
> ānandam brahmano vidvān na bibheti kadācana."
>
> ii. 4 and ii. 9.

(*Trans.*)—
Whence words return with the mind without having reached it, knowing the bliss of that Brahman, one never fears.

So, too, the Ait. Up. has very little to contribute to the subject. In one place (iii. 1–3) the Ātman is defined as consciousness (prajñāna), and then elephants, cows, men, trees, animals, etc., are called the names (nāmadheyāni) of consciousness, which is identified with Brahman (prajñānam Brahma). This means that all things exist only so far as they are my consciousness, which is a *unity*; hence the multiplicity which seems to exist independent of my consciousness is not real, but only a mere name.

The Kaṭha Up., one of the comparatively late Upaniṣads, is one of the finest productions on the subject, and contains many passages that are frequently quoted by the modern Indian Vedāntists. It is attractive moreover owing to the peculiarly fascinating and interesting legend of Naciketā, meant to expound the lore of the Ātman so as to be acceptable even to those who are tired too soon of abstract conceptions and want something to

[1] Cf. Taitt. Up. ii. 1, ii. 6, iii. 1, etc.

colour such notions. In i. 2. 5, the god of Death points out to Naciketā how the ignorant in their *avidyā* follow one another like the blind.

"avidyāyām antare vartamānāḥ svayaṃdhīrāḥ paṇḍitammanyamānāḥ,
dandramyamāṇāḥ pariyanti mūḍhāḥ andhenaiva nīyamānā yathāndhāḥ."[1]

(Cf. Muṇḍ. Up. i. 2. 8.)

(*Trans.*)—

Dwelling in the midst of darkness, "wise in their own conceit,"[2] and taking themselves to be very learned, the ignorant go round and round, staggering to and fro, like blind men led by the blind.

Such are the people who always look to the external and the immediate aspect of things and never look beyond. Imitating others blindly, they also imagine the not-self to be the self. And such people in their own ignorance regard themselves very learned (paṇḍitam-manyamānāḥ), because self-conceit is the index to shallowness of knowledge or ignorance. The more one knows, the humbler one becomes.

The most satisfactory passages, however, come later in Kaṭha ii. The one is almost identical with Bṛh. iv. 4. 19, which has already been quoted above.

[1] Cf. Muṇḍ. Up. i. 2. 8; Kaṭha Up. ii. 5; also Maitr. vii. 9. (where we have only वेष्ट्यमानाः for वर्तमानाः

[2] See S.B.E. xv., p. 8.

"yad eveha tad amutra yad amutra tad anv iha
mṛtyoḥ sa mṛtyum āpnoti ya iha nāneva paśyati."
Kaṭha Up. ii. 4. 10.

(*Trans.*)—
What is here, the same is in the next world; and what is in the next world, the same is here; he who sees here, as it were, "differences" (or "the many") goes from death to death.

Here, as we have already seen, the multiplicity is pronounced false; he who even imagines it to be true does not attain liberation. The same thought is stated in the next mantra—

"manasaiva idam avāptavyam
neha nānā asti kiñcana
mṛtyoḥ sa mṛtyum āpnoti ya iha nāneva paśyati."
Kaṭha Up. ii. 4. 11.

(*Trans.*)—
Only by the mind this is to be obtained; there is no multiplicity here whatsoever; he goes from death to death who sees any multiplicity here.

Here again the fact that there is no multiplicity whatever is particularly emphasized, hence the universe, which is the embodiment of this idea of multiplicity, is false.

The conception of the Ātman is further explained in ii. 5. 13—

"nityo anityānām cetanaś cetanānām
eko bahūnām yo vidadhāti kāmān
tam ātmasthaṃ ye 'nupaśyanti dhīrās
teṣāṃ śāntiḥ śāśvatī netareṣām." [1]

[1] Cf. Śvet. Up. vi. 13.

(*Trans.*)—

Eternal of the transient, Soul of the souls, who though one, fulfills the desires of many ; the wise who perceive Him residing in the Self, to them belongs eternal peace, not to others.

The passage distinguishes the eternal and changeless nature of the ,Ātman from the transient nature of the world, adding that only those are saved who know the Ātman, since that is the only true knowledge. All others who will hold fast to the sense of "plurality," taking the fleeting shadows for eternal realities, will never find rest and peace but will ever be rolling to and fro, confused and puzzled.

The Śvetāśvatara Up., composed still later and tinged with rather sectarian ideas, speaks of the whole cosmic illusion as capable of being removed (viśva-māyā-nivṛttiḥ) by a true knowledge of the one God Hara (i. 10). Again in iii. 8 it is said that there is no other way of conquering death except by knowing the ever-luminous Ātman. If the world were real or true, its knowledge could save people from the clutches of death. In iii. 10 it is said that only they who know the Ātman, who is beyond the Puruṣa, formless and pure, attain immortality, all others for ever plunge into misery.

That the Ātman in us is the subject of knowledge and itself is consequently unknowable is clearly brought out in—

"sa vetti vedyam na ca tasyāsti vettā tam āhur agryaṃ puruṣam mahāntam."

Śvet. Up. iii. 19.

(*Trans.*)—

He knows what is to be known, but no one knows him; they call him the first, the great Puruṣa.

In vi. 8–12 is a beautiful description of the nature of the Ātman—

"na tasya kāryaṃ karaṇaṃ na vidyate . . . netareṣām."

(*Trans.*)—

There is no effect and no cause of him, no one is seen like unto him or better; his high power is revealed as manifold, as inherent, acting as power and knowledge.

There is no master of him in the world, no ruler of him, not even a sign of him; he is the cause, the lord of the lords of the organs, and there is of him neither parent nor lord,

That only god who spontaneously covered himself, like a spider, with threads drawn from Nature (Pradhāna), grant us the imperishable Brahman.

He is the one God, hidden in all beings, all-pervading, the self within all beings, watching over all works, dwelling in all beings, the witness, the perceiver, the only one, free from qualities.

He is the one ruler of the many who are free from actions, he who makes the one seed manifold; the wise who perceive him within their self, to them belongs eternal happiness, not to others.

Śvet. Up. vi. 8–12.

An examination of the other Upaniṣads also will bear out that the conception of the sole Reality of Brahman is not missing in them. In some it is more strongly emphasized, in others it is clouded over by more realistic tendencies. This extreme idealism which refused to grant reality to the world seemed to be rather too advanced for the ordinary understanding, which could not reconcile the fact that the world was there somehow or other and it could therefore not be explained away by being called "unreal." The inherent empirical tendencies of our nature are too strong to be wholly conquered; howsoever they may be subdued, they still rise up at some time and refuse to harmonize with the metaphysical standpoint. Moreover, to the majority who are not given to step beyond the boundaries of empirical understanding such metaphysical speculations as are contained in the pure idealism of Yājñavalkya seem hardly to convey any meaning. Yet these minds are not totally to be ignored by the old sages, they must then make room for some concession to the empirical consciousness which refuses to part with the idea of the reality of the world. This could be done by granting the existence of the world and yet maintaining at the same time that the sole reality is the Ātman. This was a sort of degeneration of Idealism into Pantheism, with its doctrine "All this is Brahman" (Chān. iii. 14. 1).

It may be observed that even in one and the same passage both these tendencies are sometimes found mixed up together. The difference between the two views is rather subtle. The one—Idealism—maintains that Ātman alone is real and nothing else exists besides it; while the other—Pantheism—holds that the world does exist and yet it does not affect the principle of the sole reality of the Ātman, since it itself is nothing different from the Ātman;

both are identical, one with the other. The Ātman is called "the reality of this reality" (Satyasya satyam) in Bṛh. Up. ii. 1. 20. It is immanent in the world and pervades even the minutest particle. This view is strictly speaking untenable, yet to satisfy the gross and empirical instincts of human beings, this is the very idea that finds expression in the greater part of the Upaniṣads as a whole. The idea is chiefly represented by the Chānd. Up. The well-known condensed word *tajjalān* is significant in the following passages from the Śāṇḍilya-vidyā, and means : From Brahman is all this born (tasmāt jāyate), into Brahman all this is reabsorbed (tasmin līyate), and in Brahman all this breathes (tasmin aniti), meaning thereby that all-in-all is Brahman.

> "Sarvam khalu idaṃ Brahma
> Tajjalān iti śānta upāsīta."
>
> Chānd. Up. iii. 14. 1.

(*Trans.*)—

All this is Brahman. Let a man meditate on that as beginning, ending and breathing in It.

Further on Brahman is called "the all-effecting, all-wishing, all-smelling, all-tasting, and all this" (Ibid., iii. 14. 2 and 4).

Again, in the very interesting narration in Prapāṭhaka vi., where Uddālaka teaches his son by means of the parables of honey (vi. 9), streams (vi. 10), a large tree (vi. 11), the nyagrodha tree (vi. 12), salt (vi. 13), a blind man travelling towards the

Gāndhāra (vi. 14), etc., etc., the Ātman is spoken of as penetrating "the all"—

"sa ya eṣo aṇimā etadātmyaṃ
idam sarvaṃ tat satyaṃ sa ātmā
tat tvam asi Śvetaketo iti."

(*Trans.*)—
That which is the subtle essence, in it all that exists has its self. It is the True. It is the Self, and thou, O Śvetaketu, art it.

The following passages speak as eloquently in the same train of thought—

"Athāta Ātmādeśa Ātmā eva adhastāt
Ātmā upariṣṭāt Ātmā paścāt Ātmā
purastāt . . . Ātmā eva idaṃ
sarvaṃ iti."

Chānd. Up. vii. 25. 2.

(*Trans.*)—
Self is below, above, behind, before, right and left—Self is all this.

"eṣa vai viśvarūpa ātmā vaiśvānaraḥ."

Chānd. Up. v. 13. 1.

i.e.,
The Self which you meditate on is the Vaiśvānara Self, called Viśvarūpa.

"ya ātmā apahatapāpmā vijaro vimṛtyur viśoko vijighatso-'pipāsaḥ satyakāmaḥ satyasaṃkalpaḥ so 'nveṣṭavyaḥ sa vijijñāsitavyaḥ sa sarvāṅś ca lokān āpnoti sarvāṅsca kāmān yas tam ātmānam anuvidya vijānātīti ha prajāpatir uvāca."

Chānd. Up. viii. 7. 1.
Also viii. 7. 3.

(*Trans.*)—

Prajāpati said: "The Self which is free from sin, freed from old age, from death and grief, from hunger and thirst, which desires nothing but what is to be desired, imagines nothing but what is to be imagined, that it is which we must search out, that it is which we must try to understand. He who has searched out that Self and has understood it obtains all worlds and all desires."

"Sarvam evedam āvāṃ bhagava ātmānaṃ paśyāva ālomabhya ānakhebhyaḥ pratirūpam iti."

Chānd. Up. viii. 8. 1.

(*Trans.*)—

We both see the Self thus All, a representation even to the very hairs and nails.

We only say that the Chān. Up. may be taken to be the chief representative of this stage of thought. It of course is found in almost all the other Upaniṣads as well, and contributes the largest bulk of the whole Aupaniṣadic literature. Even the Bṛh. Up., which we have taken to be the chief exponent of pure idealism, contains many passages agreeing with the pantheistic conception.

"Brahma taṃ parādāt yo anyatra ātmano Brahma veda . . . sarvaṃ yad ayam ātmā."

Bṛh. Up. ii. 4. 6. Cf. Ibid. iv. 5. 7.

"Brahmaivedaṃ sarvam."—Bṛh. Up. ii. 5. 2.

"Brahmaitat sarvam."—Ibid. v. 3. 1.

i.e.,

All this is Brahman.

"Ayam vā ātmā sarveṣāṃ bhūtānāṃ lokaḥ."

Bṛh. Up. 1. 4. 16.

i.e.,

This Ātman is the support of all creatures.

"tad yathā rathanābhau ca . . . samarpitāḥ."
Bṛh. ii. 5. 15.

(*Trans.*)—

And as all spokes are contained in the axle and in the felly of a wheel, all beings and all those selves are contained in that Self.

"Yaḥ sarveṣu bhūteṣu tiṣṭhan . . . amṛtaḥ."—Ibid. iii. 7. 15.

He who dwells in all beings, and within all beings, whom all beings do not know, whose body all beings are, and who rules all beings within, he is thy Self, the ruler within, the "Immortal."

"Ātmani eva ātmānaṃ paśyati sarvaṃ ātmānaṃ paśyati."
Bṛh. iv. 4. 23.

The Taittir. Up. too says—

"Om iti Brahma, Om iti idaṃ sarvam."
Taitt. i. 8. 1.

The Kaṭha Up. too has the following—

"tasminl lokāḥ śritāḥ sarve."
Kaṭha ii. 5. 8. Cf. ii. 6. 1.

That the one Ātman, like the fire, the air and the sun, assumes manifold forms, forms the subject matter of Kaṭha ii. 5. 8–12.

Even the Śvetāśvatara Up., which is fundamentally theistic, contains passages like the following—

"sarvavyāpinam ātmānam," etc.
Śvet. i. 16.

"sarvānanaśirogrīvaḥ . . . śivah."
Ibid. ii. 11.

"sarvataḥ pāṇipādam . . . tiṣṭhati."
Ibid. ii. 16.

A mantra from the Puruṣa-sūkta of the R.V. is quoted as ii. 15—

> " Puruṣa evedaṃ sarvaṃ," etc.
> " viśvasya ekaṃ pariveṣṭ,itāram . . . eti."
> iv. 14 (Cf. iv. 16 and v. 13.)
> " eko devaḥ sarvabhūteṣu gūḍhaḥ . . ātmā."
> vi 11.
> " Īśāvāsyam idaṃ sarvaṃ . . . jagat."
> Īśa. 1.
> " Yas tu sarvāṇi . . . vijugupsate."
> Īśa. 6.
> " Yasmin . . anupaśyatah."
> Īṣa. 7.
> " Yasmin dyauḥ . . . setuḥ."
> Muṇḍ. ii. 2. 5.
> " Brahmaivedam . . . variṣṭham."
> Muṇḍ. ii. 2. 11.
> " Sarvam . . . catuṣpāt."
> Māṇḍ. 2.

It is not our object, however, to collect all such passages here. To multiply such instances is in no way difficult. One has only to turn over the pages of the Upaniṣads and passages tinged with this idea are sure to be found. For want of a better word we have named this conception " Pantheism." The reason why the largest portion of the Upaniṣads is pantheistic in this sense is twofold. In the first place, it is not too abstruse to escape the understanding of those who take some pains to inquire into the knowledge of the Ātman. By not denying the existence of the world it does not arouse the hostility or opposition of the general thinker. Secondly, it is not far from the real truth as given in the "pure idealism," e.g., that of Yājña-valkya. Granting as it does "a world," it boldly says that "All is the Ātman," that the only reality is the Ātman, even though the world may be taken to possess some kind of existence.

In this way for accommodating the real truth of the sole reality of the Ātman (and consequently the falsity of the world) to the empirical consciousness which refuses to part with the grosser conception of the world—an idea with which it has long been familiar—the idealist has to come down from his high pedestal and speak in words intelligible to people in general. He will, for the time being, grant that there *is* a world, but will add that "whatever *is* is the Ātman." If we analyse this form of Pantheism we find that it is not far removed from the original Idealism, since the *oneness* of the Ātman is still maintained and all this diversity in the world is said to be only a *name* depending on the Ātman for its existence; and as the *name* is unreal, it follows that even this doctrine indirectly comes to the same truth. But a further abuse of the doctrine reduces it to what we may call "the *lower* Pantheism," according to which each and every "*material*" thing is also the Ātman, the horse is the Ātman, the rider is the Ātman, the table is the Ātman, etc., so that when a man kills a snake "the Ātman has killed the Ātman" would be the vulgar way of expression; and losing sight of the original idea on which this conception is based, it is liable to be laughed at and pooh-poohed by the man in the street. But we must carefully note that this sort of Pantheism is not the essential doctrine of the Upaniṣads. It rests on a mere misunderstanding of the position, which implies that all is the Ātman, since nothing can exist (or have a *sattā*) *independent* of the Ātman. When one has realized the true nature of the Ātman, e.g., a man who is called *jīvanmukta*, he does not see anything besides the Ātman. So long as he has his body, he is within the world of imperfections and he, too, has to make some concession in saying that *this world* (which really does not exist in his view) too is not anything besides the Ātman. Such a man, being quite intoxicated with the true bliss (*ānanda*) of the Ātman, will meet all questions by the word "Ātman." Others who are still ignorant of their blindness deny that they are blind and consequently laugh at the spontaneous utterings of such a Vedāntist.

As a matter of fact, there is a strange anomaly in such a knowledge of the Ātman. The human intellect is not made to grasp the reality by its power of reason and by use of words.[1] There are limitations and imperfections inherent in it. It breaks down the moment it attempts to go beyond a certain point, its legitimate boundary. The ultimate reality refuses to be chopped up into bits in order to

[1] Cf. "naiṣā tarkeṇa matir āpaneyā"—"this knowledge cannot be reached by mere reasoning."—Kaṭha Up. i. 2, 9.

fit in with the import of language. It is self-illuminating, and to yield its meaning it demands our self-consciousness, our living will, our whole self, our whole life, but not our speech, which is after all inadequate.

In order fully to realize such truths the intellect must transcend itself, which it cannot do. Hence it has to be content with its blurred and indistinct vision.[1] But, on the other hand, *words* have to be used for communicating truth, though the moment we use them we land ourselves on quicksands. When we say, e.g., "the world is nothing but an appearance," even so we use the term "*world,*" and in so doing do suppose it to *exist.* Hence, in the interpretation of the passages of the Upaniṣads we must always confine our attention to the *spirit* underlying the text and to the motives which led the sages to unite various standpoints in one text, which may seem to be conflicting if looked at merely in the external.

The degeneration of Pure Idealism—the kernel of the Upaniṣads—did not stop here. It went so far as to turn into ultra-Realism and further on even into Atheism, Deism, etc. The natural course for Pantheism was to turn into what we may call Creationism (Cosmogonism). The identity of the Ātman and the world, though granted, was yet far

[1] On the function of the intellect compare the brilliant remarks of Prof. Bergson in his *L'Evolution Creatrice.*

from being transparent to many who had a craze for the concrete. They would argue thus: "The Ātman is One, and the world is 'the Many'; how then could the Ātman be one with the world?" The notion of *identity*, therefore, not being transparent, lost its force, and was supplanted by a still more empirical conception, viz., that of *causality*, according to which the Ātman is the cause and the world *proceeds* from it as an effect. This stage of thought prominently appears in Taitt. Up.; in this the chief passages are—

"Tasmāt etasmād vā ātmanaḥ . . . puruṣaḥ."
Taitt. ii. 1. 1.
"So 'kāmayata bahu syām . . . tat sṛṣṭvā tad evānuprāviśat." Ibid. ii. 6.
"Yato vā imāni bhūtāni . . . tad Brahmeti,."
Ibid. iii. 1.
"Sa imān lokān asṛjata."
Ait. Up. i. 2.

Such ideas are also found scattered over almost all the other Upaniṣads.[1] The most eloquent passage on the subject is the analogy of the spider and the sparks. Just as the spider goes forth from itself by means of its threads, as from the fire the tiny sparks fly out, so from this Ātman all the spirits of

[1] Cf. for example, Bṛh. i. 2. 5. (tena Ātmanā sarvam idaṃ asṛjata"), i. 4. 1, i. 4. 5, 1. 4. 10, ii. 1. 20; Chān. iii. 19. 1, vi. 2. 1, vi. 3. 2, vi. 3. 3. vii. 26. 1 ("ātmataḥ eva idam sarvaṃ"); Muṇḍ. i. 1. 7, ii. 1. 1, ii. 1. 4, ii. 1. 9; Māṇḍūkya 6; 12.

life spring forth, all worlds, all gods, all living beings (Bṛh. ii. 1. 20). The same illustrations are further set out at length in Muṇḍ. Up. i. 1. 7 and ii. 1. 1.

The one notable point in this connexion is that at this stage the Ātman who *creates* the world is identical with that who *lives in* it.[1] Brahman is the Ātman. The universal Self, the creator of the world, is not different from the individual Self within each of us. Brahman is thus the psychic principle. It is not in any way divided into so many Ātmans, but is present as a whole within each of us. It is not an aggregate of the Ātmans but the whole of the Ātman. The well-known Vedāntic formulas "*tat tvam asi,*" "That art thou" (Chānd. Up. vi. 8. 7), and "*ahaṃ brahmāsmi,*" "I am Brahman" (Bṛh. i. 4. 10), amply corroborate the idea. We have already referred to a passage (Bṛh. iii. 4, and iii. 5), where the inquiry as to the "Brahman that is within all as soul" is answered as—"It is thy soul that is within all," which as the knowing subject is itself unknowable.

Keeping in view the remoteness of the age when the authors of the Upaniṣads breathed on this earth, it strikes us as something really wonderful to grasp this relation of identity between God and man so clearly as they did. This is a thought that will ever be one of the fundamental postulates of all future metaphysics. The same has been discovered in

[1] Cf. above, e.g., "Tat sṛṣṭvā tad eva anuprāviṣat."—Taitt. Up. ii. 6.

rather a circuitous way long after by Western thinkers as well, and we believe that in spite of all the threats of materialistic, atheistic and pragmatistic movements the present century witnesses here and there, or other destructive tendencies that the future may witness, this one principle of the identity of the Ātman with the Absolute will ever remain unshaken. Take away this principle and you destroy all metaphysics worth the name.

Now, the adaptation of the higher truth to the empirical understanding went still further. This identity of the creative principle with our inner self was not so attractive to the hard-headed men accustomed to look always to the external. They failed to understand how the great and infinite Brahman who created the world could be the same as the little Ātman within us of the size of a thumb (anguṣṭhamātraḥ). "Oh," they would say, "the proclaimed identity is not true, it is meaningless to us; even if it be true, it is beyond us to understand it." This necessitated a further concession to suit the innate empirical tendencies of such people—in fact, all of us as men do have such tendencies, and our inefficient intellect fails to grasp this higher truth—and it was held that the Ātman who creates the world may be *distinguished* from that who is within us. The former was called the *Paramātman* (the Great Ātman) or the Īśvara (the Governor), and the latter, the *Jīvātman* (the individual Ātman). Cosmogonism thus paved the way to Theism. The distinction between the two Ātmans begins to appear in the Kāṭhaka Up., and continues in some of the later Upaniṣads. Even as early as in the Bṛh. Up. some tendencies towards this position are noticeable :—

> "At the bidding of this imperishable one, O Gārgi, sun and moon are held asunder," etc.
>
> Bṛh. iii. 8. 9.
>
> "Here within the heart is a cavity, therein he dwells, the lord of the Universe, the governor of the Universe, the chief of the Universe ; he is the bridge that holds asunder these worlds, and prevents them from clashing together."
>
> Bṛh. iv. 4. 22.

This is not yet *Theism*, but a preparation to it. Real Theism begins with a contrast between Brahman and the individual Self. This first appears in the Kaṭha Up., where the distinction between these two Ātmans is likened to that between light and shadow—

> "Ṛtaṃ pibantau sukṛtasya loke
> guhāṃ praviṣṭau parame parārdhe
> chāyātapau brahmavido vadanti
> pañcāgnayo ye ca triṇāciketāḥ."
>
> Kaṭha i. 3. 1.

(*Trans.*)—

The two, enjoying the fruits of their good deeds, being lodged in the cavity of the seat of the Supreme, the knowers of Brahman call shadow and light, as also do those who maintain five fires and have thrice propitiated the Naciketa fire."

Kaṭha i. 3. 1.

The chief exponent at this level of thought is the Śvetāśvatara Up., in which though the original identity of Brahman and the individual Ātman is not denied, yet a distinction is clearly drawn out, e.g., in the following chief passage—

> "Ajām ekāṃ lohitaśuklakṛṣṇām
> bahvīḥ prajāḥ sṛjamānāṃ sarūpāḥ,
> ajo hy eko juṣamāṇo 'nuśete
> jahāty enāṃ bhuktabhogām ajo 'nyaḥ.
>
> "dvā suparṇā sayujā sakhāyā
> samānaṃ vṛkṣaṃ pariṣasvajāte,
> tayor anyaḥ pippalaṃ svādv atti
> anaśnann anyo 'bhicākaśīti.
>
> "samāne vṛkṣe puruso nimagnaḥ
> anīśayā śocati muhyamānaḥ,
> juṣṭam yadā paśyaty anyam īśam
> asya mahimānam iti vītaśokah."
>
> Śvet. Up. iv. 5, 6, 7.

Passages exhibiting a Pantheistic and Idealistic trend of thought are not wanting in this Up. also. These stages are set down side by side to suit the variety of human understanding.[1] The type of theism we have indicated here, viz., that which makes Brahman a personal god and distinguishes Him from the individual soul, is perhaps most acceptable to the masses, but we do not hesitate to call Theism a lower conception than the Pure Idealism sketched above, we call it a mere pictorial way of

[1] In Śvet. Up. i. 6, the distinction spoken of above is explained as illusory. The theistic tinge comes in when it is said that the removal of this illusion depends on the grace of the Lord.

representing a truth in a more concrete and simple way to let it harmonize with the common understanding, repulsed by " abstract " truths. These people want some *concrete* idea, which will give a colouring to their imagination whenever they venture to think about the origin of the world in which they live and move, and it is Theism which they will welcome instinctively.

But how long and how far could such a separation between the Lord (Īśvara) and the soul exist? The natural consequence was a further degeneration, which in a clever way solved the dualism by striking out one of its components, viz., the former. One had to give way, and the empirical instinct in man would rather believe in the existence of the soul than of the Īśvara, which seemed more remote and was not witnessed by the soul. In this struggle therefore the conception of the Paramātman was ousted. There remained only the individual soul (named now the Puruṣa) and the external " real " world (called the Prakṛti). This is known as the Sāṅkhya standpoint, and may be called Atheism for want of a better word. It may also be added very briefly that the progressive realism further manifested itself in two more aspects.

The first was the denial even of the individual soul. The existence of the world could not be denied, since it is perceived; but one could doubt the reality of the soul. Let us call those who did so " *Apsychists.*" This denial of the soul and the belief in an external world only, which was more or less a stream of perceptions, changing and momentary, found its place in Buddhism. The second aspect was the furthermost degeneration into gross materialism, which would even rob Buddhism of all idealistic leanings (or tendency). Only matter exists, and what is called mind is a mere product of it. Perception is the only way to knowledge, and all else is unreal. Such thoughts constituted the School of Cārvāka.

Here we may stop so far as the degeneration of the Pure Idealism is concerned; it was impossible for this degeneration to go further than the Cārvākas, who are regarded as the extreme realists of Indian philosophy.

The short account we have sketched above on this subject may perhaps seem to be a digression from our subject proper, but even if so, it is quite intentional, since we believe that it may help to present our Idealism in its relation to other stages of thought, most of which are themselves found in the Upaniṣads. So long as these are not viewed in their mutual relation and coherence, it is not to be wondered that one may accuse the Upaniṣads of manifest contradictions. But a general view of the way in which the basic truth of the Upaniṣads, the doctrine of the sole reality of Brahman, degenerated, or "developed" from another standpoint, into the more realistic stages of thought in order to adapt itself to the empirical tendencies innate in all of us may bring home to us a better idea of the teachings of these treatises in general, and of the place of the pure Idealism (which may otherwise be named as the conception of Māyā) in Indian thought as a whole.

We shall presently see how the great Śaṅkara synthesises all these forms of thought into a single whole, in which each has a proper place beside the other, and how he saves the Pure Idealism by the help of the Śruti as well as reason. But we must not anticipate him. Before we discuss his Advaitism and what he has to say on the theory of Māyā, we have to refer to the philosophy of another great Advaitist, *Gauḍapāda*. This name is in no way to be identified with the author of a commentary on Īśvara Kṛṣṇa's Sāṅkhya Kārikā.[1] The Advaitist Gauḍapāda was the teacher of Govinda, the teacher of Śaṅkara. He has left to us one of the most wonderful expositions of the fundamentals of Advaitism, called "Kārikās on the Māṇḍūkya Upaniṣad."

[1] On this point compare the views of Deussen, *System des Vedānta*, p. 26; Garbe, *Sāṅkhya-Philosophie*, p. 61; Weber, *Ak. Vorl., Zweite Auflage*, pp. 178, 254, 260; Hall, *Contributions towards an Index*, p. 86; Gough, *Philosophy of the Upaniṣads*, p. 240; Max Müller, *Six Systems of Indian Philosophy*, p. 292; Colebrooke, *Miscellaneous Essays*, 1837, vol. i., p. 95, 104, 233; Wilson, *Text and English Translation of the Sāṅkhya-Kārikā*, p. 257; Windischmann, *Śaṅkara*, Bonn, 1830, p. 85, etc.

I am indebted for these references to Max Walleser's *Der ältere Vedānta*, Heidelberg, 1910, p. 1.

The nature of our subject requires us to examine this work in some detail, instead of simply speaking of it as such. The Kārikā is divided into four parts, and as already observed, each of these is looked upon as having the authority of an Upaniṣad. The four parts are named: *Āgama*, *Vaitathya*, *Advaita* and *Alātaśānti*. The first, which in its subject-matter is chiefly based on the Māṇdūkya Up., discusses the nature and significance of the secret syllable "Om," and as it hangs mainly on the Śruti or the *Āgama* (i.e., the Veda) it is called *Āgama*. The second explains by means of argument how the world, characterized as it is by duality, is false (vaitathya), hence it is named *Vaitathya*. In the third are refuted the accusations against the Advaita view and then the real standpoint is maintained by reason; hence it is called *Advaita*. In the fourth are refuted all the arguments which, while attacking Advaitism, themselves prove contradictory; and then a calm is restored and the final word is spoken on the sole reality of the Ātman and the falsity of all else. This part is therefore aptly termed *Alāta-śānti*, which means the extinction of a firebrand. As a stick burning at one end is waved round quickly in the air, it seems to create a circle of fire (alāta-cakra), which does not really exist, so it is with the multiplicity only appearing but not existing really. The example may sound rather unfamiliar to Western ears, but it must not be forgotten that it appeals most vividly to the Indian. The sport known as *Alāta-cakra* is a very common sight in the streets, where little boys play in the evening after having finished their daily school-task.

The first part, as already remarked, being based on the Upaniṣad, Gauḍapāda could give an unchecked flight to his thoughts only in the other three parts. These are therefore more important for our purpose. We here give a brief summary of the Advaitism of this great teacher, which is permeated with the conception of "Māyā."

Boldly and truly Gauḍapāda asserts the world does not exist in reality; hence this Māyā cannot be literally removed or destroyed even. All this is mere appearance, in sooth it is "Advaita." In other words, the metaphysical truth is that the world does not exist, the multiplicity is false, hence being not a reality it does not stand in need of removal (i. 17). Nobody ever MADE "*māyā*"; it is *not* a reality, hence it is meaningless to speak of it as "to be removed." When the highest truth is realized the illusion itself is destroyed (i. 18).

In the second part Gauḍapāda explains the unreality (vaitathya) of all multiplicity by showing that the world which people call real is no more real than a dream-world. The two worlds are alike in this respect, the only difference is that the waking-world is *external*, while the dream-world is *internal*. But as witnessed by the same self they are the same, both being within the body in a subtle form (ii. 1). Sankara explains this stanza logically thus—

Proposition (*pratijñā*)—
Objects seen in the waking world are unreal.
(jāgraddṛśyānāṃ bhāvānāṃ vaitathyam.)
Reason (*hetu*):
Because they are capable of being seen.
(dṛśyamānatvāt.)
Illustration (*dṛṣṭānta*):
Like the objects seen in a dream.
(svapnadṛśyabhāvavat.)
Argument (*hetūpanaya*):
As in a dream the objects seen are false, so too in waking, their capability of being seen is the same.
(Yathā tatra svapne dṛśyānāṃ bhāvānāṃ vaitathyaṃ tathā jāgarite 'pi dṛśyatvam aviśiṣṭam iti.)
Conclusion (*nigamana*):
Therefore in the waking condition too they (the objects seen) are false (tasmāj jāgarite 'pi vaitathyaṃ smṛtam iti).

Though, on account of being internal and in a subtle condition, the phenomena of dream are different from those of waking, yet (the fact remains) that their being seen (*dṛśyamānatva*) and their consequent futility (or falsity, *vaitathya*) of presentation, are common to both. In ii. 5 the same is finally enunciated.

From an analysis of our experience we find that what is naught at the beginning and end is necessarily so at the middle too. For instance, the mirage is nothing in the beginning, since it never was a mirage, so too it is nothing at the end, since it never existed; hence it could not have any tertiary existence. The objects of our waking experience are finally of the same class as the mirage, hence possess no independent existence whatever. It is only the ignorant, says Śaṅkara, who regard the image in the glass as real (ii. 6). But it may be objected that the two phenomena in question are not quite similar, consequently to deduce the futility of either from its similarity to the other is not valid. The objects seen in dreams are not copies of those seen in the waking condition. In dreams one is not always having experience in harmony with the objects of sense, but sees objects transcending the limits of experience. For instance, one sees objects which are never found in the waking condition and has strange experiences, such as finding oneself with eight hands sitting on an elephant with four heads, and so forth. All these are not copies of anything unreal, hence they are real in themselves. But it may be replied that all this rests on a misunderstanding. That which is supposed to transcend the limits of experience in dreams is not an absolute reality in itself but only a condition of the cogniser conditioned by that state. As those living in heaven, such as Indra and others, have a thousand eyes, etc., by the very conditions of their existence, so the transcending of the limits of experience is the very condition of the cogniser in dreams. Hence, as the rope, the serpent, the mirage, etc., being merely the conditions of the cogniser, are unreal, so the transcendent phenomena of dreams are only a result of the condition of the cogniser, and, therefore, unreal [1] (ii. 8). Further,

[1] See Dvivedi, Māṇḍūkya Upaniṣad, etc., trans. p. 42.

it must be noted that it is only from a relative standpoint that dreams are spoken of as unreal and the waking condition as real. Truly speaking, both are unreal. Even as to the phenomena in dreams, though the whole of them are known to be unreal, none the less the facts arrange themselves under reality and unreality (ii. 9. 10).

Now, if the whole of our experience in both the waking and the dreaming conditions is pronounced to be an illusion, well might an objector come forward to say—" Who is then the knower or creator of experience ? " (ii. 11). If you say " none " you at once destroy the reality of the *Ātman*, which would be laying an axe at the very foot of all Vedānta, since the conception of the reality of the Ātman is the very life of it.

The Ātman, we reply, is the cogniser of experience. He is himself the cogniser and the cognised. He imagines himself by himself, i.e., brings about the variety of experience by himself. It all subsists also in himself through the power of Māyā. This is the last word of the Vedānta on this subject (ii. 12).

Our waking experiences are as much an illusion as those of dreams. For the phenomena of dreams are for the time as real as those of waking. The difference is not in the nature of any of these experiences as such ; it is caused only by the instruments of cognition (ii. 15).

The Ātman is the only reality. As the rope, whose

nature is not known as such at that time, is imagined in the dark to be a snake, a line of water, a stick, or any one of numerous similar things, so is the Ātman imagined to be the variety of experience, *Jīva*, *Prāṇa*, etc. (ii. 17). All illusion vanishes when a complete knowledge of the rope is attained, such knowledge persisting for all time. So too is confirmed the right knowledge that all is one, viz., the Ātman (ii. 12). It is only the power of illusion which makes us imagine the Ātman as the variety of numberless visible objects (ii. 19).

As dream and illusion are entirely unreal, though actually perceived, so is the cosmos an illusion, an unreality, though experienced as real. Only the ignorant regard such illusions as real. The Scriptural texts amply set forth the unreality of the cosmos (ii. 31). The absolute truth is that there is, as a matter of fact, no dissolution, no creation, none in bondage, no pupilage, none desirous of liberation, none liberated. In other words, when it is established that the Ātman alone is real and all duality is an illusion, it follows that all that forms the subject of experience, whether derived from ordinary intercourse or from sacred texts, is mere illusion. In the absolute sense of the word, therefore, " Destruction " is impossible. So too creation, etc. (ii. 32). The Ātman is ever free from all imaginations and is never in relation to any conditions. He is the negation of the phenomenal, because of his essential nature of unity. But only the sages, free from attachment, fear, anger, and well versed in the Scriptures, are able to perceive this truth (ii. 35).

Having realized the Ātman, the wise man should be in the world like a block of inert matter, i.e., being perfectly unmoved and unattached to the duality. In this way, though still being within the world, he will transcend it; from the point of view of this world therefore, he will be a sort of block of dead matter (ii. 36). This consciousness of the self-realization of the *Ātman* should never cease (ii. 38).

The third part ("Advaita") begins with the idea that the Ātman, though appearing to give birth to the multiplicity of things all about us, is not in the least affected by any such thing (iii. 2). Multiplicity is only due to self-imposed and imagined limitations. The individuation of the Ātman into the Jīvas is not a process of division. The division appears as real. For instance, the Ātman, being indivisible and all-pervading, may be compared to ether (ākāśa). It is not different from the ether enclosed in a jar; the enclosure being destroyed, the limited *ākāśa* merges into *mahākāśa.* So is Jīva merged in the Ātman on the dissolution of the self-imposed adjuncts [1] (iii. 3. 4). Differences are only in form, capacity, name, etc., but that does not imply any real difference in *ākāśa* itself. This illustration may fully apply to Jīva (iii. 6). As, again, *ākāśa* intercepted by a "jar" is neither a part nor an evolved

[1] On this compare Śaṅkara on ii. 1. 14 below.

effect of *ākāśa*, so is Jīva neither a part nor an evolved effect of the Ātman (iii. 7).

The Śāstras praise the unity of the Ātman, demonstrated by reason and borne out by Scriptures, while they censure manifoldness or separateness. The separation between Jīva and the Ātman is only assumed and need only be taken in a metaphysical sense (iii. 13. 14). Again, the distinctionless Ātman, eternal and unborn, appears with distinctness under so many finite and mortal forms simply through māyā ; for, if the distinctions were real, the immortal would in that case necessarily become mortal, which on the very face of it is impossible, since a thing cannot be changed into anything of quite an opposite nature (iii. 19. 21).

The Ātman is ever unborn and one. It does not convert itself into the world of experience. If it did, it would go on taking birth after birth *ad infinitum*, thus precluding all possibility of liberation. The birth of worlds is possible only through māyā. Nothing can be actually born of the Ātman. It may only be *supposed* to give birth to things, like the rope to the snake, etc., but not in reality (iii. 27).

Again, *Asat* (non-existence), cannot be taken as the cause or source of everything. The son of a barren women is a concept without meaning, never to be realized in reality or even in illusion (iii. 28). All duality is nothing but a creation of the mind, since it stands or falls with the mind (iii. 31).

The fourth part, called *Alāta-śānti*, i.e., "Quenching the Fire-brand," is the final pronouncement of Gauḍapāda, which is intended to destroy the illusion of the "fire-brand." The relation between cause and effect is examined, and it is shown how it breaks down while applying to the Ātman (iv. 11–19). Nothing is produced either of itself or by something else, nor, in fact, is anything produced, whether it be being, non-being, or both (iv. 22). The various theories held by the Vijñānavādins, the Nihilists, etc., are false (iv. 28). Those who maintain the reality of the world must not forget to realize that the world, being without a beginning, cannot, in reason, be shown to have an end. Nothing which is beginningless is non-eternal. So also is it impossible to prove the eternity of salvation, realized only at the moment of its knowledge, and therefore having a beginning (iv. 30). That which is naught at the beginning and at the end, cannot exist in the present; objects are all like ordinary illusions, though regarded as real (iv. 31).

Thought—all-peace and one, the ever-unborn, immovable and immaterial, appears as admitting of creative motion and material existence. *Sat* is unborn and eternal, still it appears to pass into birth, etc. (iv. 45). Thus neither is the mind produced nor are the objects; those who know this are never deluded into a false consciousness (iv. 46). As motion makes a fire-brand appear straight, crooked, etc., so motion makes thought appear as perceiver, perceived and the like (iv. 47). The fire-brand is not itself affected by its appearance and is ever unborn, its motion being unreal; so is thought unaffected by appearance, and is ever unborn, its apparent motion being an illusion (iv. 48). The appearances of the fire-brand in motion are not brought into it from without; and they do not appear in any other place when it is at rest, though they do not appear to enter it (iv. 49). The same applies to thought. When thought is in motion like the fire-brand, appearances do not come from without; also they do not go out anywhere beyond the motion, neither do they enter thought. They are always indescribable because of their defiance to the relation of cause and effect (iv. 51–52). So long as one has faith in causality, one sees the world eternally present; this faith being destroyed, the world is nowhere (iv. 56). Duality consisting of subject and object is a creation of the external senses (iv. 87). Those who always hold fast to "duality" never perceive the truth (iv. 94). The treatise ends with a salutation to the Absolute after having realized it, such an attitude being justified from the standpoint or relativity and experience (iv. 100).

In this brief survey we have attempted to show how the sage Gauḍapāda establishes a thoroughgoing monist's position, calling the whole world of experience as false as the dream-world, analysing the notions of existence and reality, refuting the idea of causality, and even giving a psychological genesis of appearances. The conception of Māyā was by him developed into a more or less systematic whole, which was afterwards still further elaborated by Śaṅkara. The general sketch we have here given of Gauḍapāda's idealism will suffice for our purpose, and without dwelling on it any more we now pass on to the final synthesis of the doctrine in Śaṅkara. In passing, it may be observed that there is hardly any teacher of note, between the times of Gauḍapāda and Śaṅkara, who contributed anything worth the name to the development of the idea of Māyā. There may perhaps have been some, but unfortunately their names have not come down to us. We purposely omit in this chapter the discussion of Bādarāyaṇa's Sūtras for reasons which are not without justification. The Sūtras, as they stand apart from Śaṅkara's commentary or any other exposition of them, may hardly be said to yield one definite, fixed and indisputable interpretation, either in favour of or against any doctrine of the Vedānta. Śaṅkara, Rāmānuja, and many other expositors, including some of the very modern ones, have respectively attempted to wield the Sūtras as weapons for the defence and support of their own interpretations and conceptions of the chief metaphysical problems. None of them is *prima facie* open to reconciliation with the others. In face of such facts it would indeed be worth the trouble to go deeply into the problem, viz., how far can the Sūtras as such be made to give any definite interpretation and meaning ? As far as we are aware, nobody has yet gone into these details, and it would certainly be no mean subject for further research. Our present purpose, however, precludes us from undertaking this additional task here, and even if any such suggestions were brought forward, they would not materially affect the position of the question at issue. Personally, we are inclined to take Śaṅkara as the best and the most satisfactory exponent of Bādarāyaṇa's views on the Vedānta problems. We do endorse the view that to Śaṅkara was handed down the tradition in its genuineness. But dogmatizing on such points is of no use, and one is at liberty to hold whatever view one likes on matters incapable of any direct proof. Hence we now pass on to a discussion of Śaṅkara's contributions on the question of Māyā.

As an interpreter of the Vedic tradition and the Vedānta of the Upaniṣads, Śaṅkara found himself in a difficult and peculiar situation. He observed, on the one hand, the different ways of explaining the problem of Reality in these philosophical treatises: all of them as such could not be taken as ultimately true. Their seeming contradictions, even as such, could not be merely ignored. Yet on the other hand, all these were to him *Vaidic* (i.e., based on the Śruti), and hence revelations of the Divine Truth, which by the force of his tradition he had to accept. He noticed, e.g., that the purely metaphysical standpoint of Yājñavalkya was at any rate quite incompatible with the less advanced views —the later stages in the degeneration of pure Idealism, which we have briefly described above—and yet each of these phases of thought claimed validity on the basis of a certain Śruti. He was thus in a way on the horns of a dilemma, from which he found an escape with caution and wisdom, acting quite in the spirit of all great "synthesisers" of thought. In attaining such syntheses, sometimes a clean sweep has to be made, and Śaṅkara was not wanting in the courage for this. He asserted that knowledge is of two kinds: *parā* (higher) and *aparā* (lower), the former referring to the unqualified Brahman, and the latter including all else; that is to say, *parā vidyā* means only the highest metaphysical Vedānta such as is given in the pure idealism of Yājñavalkya, Gauḍapāda, etc. The other parts of the Upaniṣads, which deal with more realistic or empirical views, as well as the whole ritual canon of the Vedas, with its things commanded and forbidden under promise of reward and punishment in another world, the Smṛtis, etc., are all labelled as *aparā vidyā*. To include the Vedas under this latter head was certain to offend the masses, yet Śaṅkara took this course, which was indeed essential for his synthesis. The thought that the empirical view of nature is unable to lead us to a final solution of the being of things, was occupying the central position in his mind. "More closely examined," as Deussen [1]

[1] *System des Vedānta*, chap. ii.

has so eloquently pointed out, "this thought is even the root of all metaphysics, so far as without it no metaphysics can come into being or exist." This thought is the great dynamic force in Śaṅkara, and it is this that led him to base the whole of his system—as reflected in the Śārīrakabhāṣya [1]—on the fundamental concept of the illusory nature of all our empirical and physical knowledge and the true nature of the higher metaphysics. That is the reason why he starts with an examination into the erroneous transference of the things and relations of the objective world to the inner soul, the Self, which leads to the idea of *avidyā*. This thought, which forms the introduction to his epoch-making book, in a way gives an idea of his whole system, and we could not do better than state the whole position in his own words, which, if well understood, are sure to furnish a key to Śaṅkara's whole Advaitism. Object (viṣaya) and Subject (viṣayin), he says at the beginning of his work, indicated by the "Thou" (the not-I) and the "I," are of a nature as opposed as are darkness and light. If it is certain that the being of the one is incompatible with the being of the other, it follows so much the more that the qualities of the one also do not exist in the other. Hence it follows that the transfer (superimposition,

[1] In his Introduction he defines it as "atasmin tadbuddhiḥ," i.e., "supposing a thing to be what it is not actually.

adhyāsa) of the object denoted by the "Thou" and its qualities to the pure spiritual object indicated by the "I," and conversely, the transfer of the subject and its qualities to the object, are logically false. Yet in mankind this procedure, resting on a false knowledge pairing together the true and the untrue, is inborn or natural (*naisargika*), so that they transfer the being and qualities of the one to the other, not separating object and subject, although they are absolutely different, and so saying, for example, "This am I," "That is mine," etc. This transference thus made the wise term *Avidyā* (ignorance), and, in contradistinction to it, they call the accurate determination of the true nature of things ("the being-in-itself" of things, *vastusvarūpam*) *Vidyā* (knowledge). If this be so, it follows that that to which a similar false transfer is thus made, is not in the slightest degree affected by any want or excess caused thereby.

All this goes to show that the final reason of the false empirical concept is to be sought in the nature of our cognitive faculty, as this passage clearly brings out the unalterableness of the Self. From this it may rightly be inferred "that the ground of the erroneous empirical concept is to be sought for solely in the knowing subject; in this subject the *avidyā*, as repeatedly asserted,[1] is innate (*nai-*

[1] Cf. Śaṅkara's Śārīrakabhāṣya, Bibl. Ind., p. 10, l. 1, p. 21. 7, 807. 12.

sargika) ; its cause is a wrong perception ;[1] its being is a wrong conception.[2]

Now we proceed to an examination of some of the typical passages[3] in Śaṅkara which sum up his whole position with respect to Māyā.

One of the most important passages, which sums up Śaṅkara's view, viz., Brahman alone is the reality (" Brahmavyatirekeṇa kāryajātasyābhāvaḥ "[4]) and is found in his commentary on ii. 1. 14 (" tadananyatvam ārambhaṇaśabdādibhyaḥ ") runs thus—

" The effect is this manifold world consisting of ether and so on ; the cause is the highest Brahman. Of the effect it is understood that in reality it is non-different from the cause, i.e., has no existence apart from the cause. How so ? " On account of the scriptural word 'origin' (ārambhaṇa ") and others." The word " ārambhaṇa " is used in connexion with a simile, in a passage undertaking to show how through the knowledge of one thing everything is known, viz., Chānd. Up. vi. 1. 4 : " As, O good one ! by one clod of clay all that is made of clay is known, the modification being a name merely

[1] Cf. Ibid. p. 9. 3. " It is mithyā-jñāna-nimitta."

[2] " mithyā-pratyaya-rūpa," p. 21. 7. See Deussen, *System*, ch. ii.

[3] In going through the whole book, the passages which appeared to be typical on this point are found in the commentary on i. 1. 9, i. 1. 20, i. 3. 19, i. 4.3, i. 4. 6, ii. 1. 14, ii. 1. 31, ii. 1. 33, ii. 2. 2, ii. 2. 4, ii. 2. 7, ii. 2. 9.

[4] *Vedāntasūtras with Śaṅkara's Commentary*, Bibl. Ind., Calcutta, 1863, vol. i. p. 444, ll. 11–12.

which has its origin in speech, while the truth is that it is clay merely, thus," etc. The meaning of this passage is, that if there is known a lump of clay which really and truly is nothing but clay, there are known thereby likewise all things made of clay, such as jars, dishes, pails, and so on, all of which agree in having clay for their true nature. For these modifications and effects are names only, exist through or originate from speech only, while in reality there exists no such thing as a modification. In so far as they are names (individual effects distinguished by names) they are untrue; in so far as they are clay they are true. This parallel instance is given with reference to Brahman; applying the phrase "*vācārambhaṇa*" to the case illustrated by the instance quoted, we understand that the entire body of effects has no existence apart from Brahman. Later on again the text, after having declared that fire, water and earth are the effects of Brahman, maintains that the effects of these three elements have no existence apart from them (Chānd. Up. vi. 4. 1). Other sacred texts [1] also, whose purpose is to intimate the unity of the Self, are to be quoted here in accordance with "the others" of the Sūtra. On any other assumption it would not be possible to maintain that by the knowledge of one thing everything becomes known. We therefore must adopt

[1] Cf. Chānd. vi. 8. 7; vii. 25. 2; Bṛhad. ii. 4. 6; iv. 4. 25; Muṇḍ. ii. 2. 11.

the following view :—In the same way as those parts of ethereal space which are limited by jars and water-pots are not really different from the universal ethereal space, and as the water of a mirage is not really different from the surface of the desert—for the nature of that water is that it is seen in one moment and has vanished in the next, and, moreover, it is not to be perceived by its own nature (i.e., apart from the surface of the desert)—so this manifold world with its objects of enjoyment, enjoyers, etc., has no existence apart from Brahman."[1]

A little further, replying to the pluralists' objections " that if we acquiesce in the doctrine of absolute unity—

(1) The ordinary means of right knowledge, perception, etc., become invalid, because the absence of manifoldness deprives them of their objects ;

(2) All the texts embodying injunctions and prohibitions will lose their purport if the distinction on which their validity depends does not really exist ;

(3) The entire body of doctrines which refer to final release will collapse, if the distinction of teacher and pupil on which it depends is not real,"

Śaṅkara says—

[1] Śaṅkara on ii. 1. 14, *Bibl. Ind.*, p. 444–445. See Thibaut's Translation, S.B.E., i., p. 320–321. Cf. Deussen, *Die Sūtras des Vedānta*, p. 281.

"These objections, we reply, do not damage our position, because the entire complex of phenomenal existence is considered as true as long as the knowledge of Brahman being the Self of all has not arisen; just as the phantoms of a dream are considered to be true until the sleeper awakes. For as long as a person has not reached the true knowledge of the unity of the Self, so long it does not enter his mind that the world of effects with its means and objects of right knowledge and its results of actions is untrue; he rather, in consequence of his ignorance, looks on mere effects as forming part of and belonging to his Self, forgetful of Brahman being in reality the Self of all. Hence as long as true knowledge does not present itself, there is no reason why the ordinary course of secular and religious activity should not hold on undisturbed. The case is analogous to that of a dreaming man, who in his dream sees manifold things, and up to the moment of waking is convinced that his ideas are produced by real perception without suspecting the perception to be a merely apparent one."

These eloquent passages speak for themselves, and hardly call for any further discussion. Here Śaṅkara by making use of appropriate analogies endorses and develops the same metaphysical truth as was held by Yājñavalkya, Gauḍapāda, etc. The unity of the Self is the maxim, and it is defended against the charge of its stopping all possibilities of activity, exertion, etc., in the world. There are two other similes used by Śaṅkara in describing the nature of Brahman, and before we refer to his other passages let us see what he says in his comments on ii. 1. 9—

"With regard to the case referred to in the Śruti-passages, we refute the assertion of the cause being affected by the effects and its qualities by showing that the latter are the mere fallacious super-impositions of nescience, and the very same argument holds good with reference to reabsorption also. We can quote other examples in favour of our doctrine. As the magician is not at any time affected by the magical illusion produced by himself, because it is unreal, so the highest Self is not affected by the illusory visions of his dream because they do not accompany the waking state and the state of dreamless sleep; so the one permanent witness of the three states (the highest Self) is not touched by the mutually exclusive three states. For that the highest Self appears in those three states is a mere illusion, not more substantial than the snake for which the rope is mistaken in the darkness. On this point teachers knowing the true tradition of the Vedānta[1] have declared: 'When the individual soul which is held in the bonds of slumber by the beginningless Māyā awakes, then it knows the eternal, sleepless, dreamless non-duality.'"[2]

We see then that Śaṅkara is very anxious to convince us of the truth of his doctrine, and to explain it in a picturesque way for the sake of the uninitiated, makes use of some very appropriate similes, among which are—

(1) The rope and the snake.[3]
(2) The magician or juggler (māyāvin) and his jugglery.
(3) The desert and the mirage.
(4) The dreamer and the dream.

The last of these has been already made use of

[1] Ref. Gauḍapāda.
[2] Gauḍapāda, *Kārikā*, i. 16.
[3] See also Śaṅkara on i. 3. 19.

exhaustively by Gauḍapāda. It has been shown that experiences of the waking condition are no less unreal than those of dream. Both are illusions alike. Śaṅkara works out the same idea in the passage quoted above, and only touching upon it briefly leads us to see that the Ātman is not affected in any way by the assumed existence of the world. If we just think for a moment about the subject of dreams, we perceive that we can hold without any fear of contradiction that—

(1) The dream-state is as real as the waking state so long as the dream lasts—i.e., so long as the consciousness to distinguish the dream as such from the waking condition has not arisen.[1]

(2) But as the illusory nature of a dream is determined only on waking up from the sleep, which prepared the way for it; so too on acquiring a knowledge of the Ātman—the sole reality—waking up from the slumber of ignorance, the truth that the world is an illusion is clearly perceived.

(3) It is only "relatively" speaking that we say "the dream-world is *unreal*" and "the waking world is *real*"; strictly speaking

[1] Mr. F. H. Bradley, the well-known author of *Appearance and Reality*, once told us that there could be no difficulty whatever on speculative grounds in holding this position. Socrates (in Plato) discussed the same view, and Tennyson said, "Dreams are true while they last."

both are unreal. The difference does not lie in the very nature of things, since the fact stated above under the first head is indubitably true.

If the ultimate reality is nothing but the One Ātman, how is it that we perceive multiplicity here? How do we find so many Jīvas? Are they different from the Absolute, or are they *parts* of it, or what? What is this differentiation due to? What is the principle of individuation? To all such questions Śaṅkara answers with the aid of the theory of Māyā. All these differences are only due to the imposition of name (nāma) and form (rūpa). Here he says in the course of his exposition on ii. 1. 14—

"Belonging to the Self, as it were, of the omniscient Lord, there are *name* and *form*, the creations of *Avidyā*, not to be defined either as being Brahman nor different from it, the germs of the entire expanse of the phenomenal world, called in Śruti and Smṛti the power of Illusion (māyāśaktiḥ) or Prakṛti. . . . Thus the Lord depends as Lord upon the limiting adjuncts of name and form, the products of Avidyā; . . . while in reality none of these qualities belong to the Self whose true nature is cleared, by right knowledge, from all adjuncts whatever. . . . In this manner the Vedānta-texts declare that for him who has reached the state of truth and reality the whole apparent world does not exist."

Again, on i. 3. 19, refuting the view that the individual soul is not identical with the Universal, Śaṅkara remarks—

"Some are of opinion that the individual soul, as such,

is real. To refute all these speculators who obstruct the way to the complete intuition of the unity of the Self this Śārīraka-Śāstra has been set forth, whose aim it is to show that there is only one highest Lord ever unchanging, who is cognition, and who by means of nescience (avidyā) manifests himself in various ways, just as a juggler appears in different shapes by means of his magical powers."

The difference of Jīva and Brahman is again set forth in the same place as being only due to *avidyā*—

"avidyākalpitaṃ lokaprasiddhaṃ jīvabhedam."
Bibl. Ind., p. 269.[1]

Saṅkara's greatness as a synthesiser of Advaitism lay, as we have already remarked, in two things: first, in the important and useful distinction he drew between "*parā*" and "*aparā*" *vidyā*, which gave a rational explanation of all the so-called conflicting statements in the Vedas, etc.; secondly, in his emphasis on the distinction between the empirical (vyāvahārikī) and metaphysical (pāramārthikī) existence, which was in some way an improvement upon Gauḍapāda. The distinction is implicitly observed in the Upaniṣads and in Gauḍapāda's Kārikās too, but nowhere is it more clearly and em-

[1] On the same subject compare pp. 267, 342, 353, 454, 455, 488, 491, 507, 518. In general for the doctrine of Avidyā compare p. 98, l. 8, 112. 3, 182. 12, 185. 12, 199. 5, 205. 10, 343. 4, 360. 2, 433. 13, 452. 2, 455. 4, 473. 17, 483. 6, 507. 1, 660. 10, 680. 12, 682. 3, 689. 1, 690. 5, 692. 14, 787. 13, 804. 1, 807. 11, 837. 2, 860. 15, 1,056. 1, 1,132. 10, 1,133. 12, 1,133. 15.

phatically brought out than in Śaṇkara. For instance, he remarks on page 488—

"All empiric action is true, so long as the knowledge of the Self is not reached, just as the action in dreams before awaking takes place. As long in fact as the knowledge of unity with the true Self is not reached, one does not have a consciousness of the unreality of the procedure connected with standards and objects of knowledge and fruits of works, but every creature, under a designation of 'I' and 'mine, mistakes mere transformations for the Self and for characteristics of the Self, and on the other hand leaves out of consideration their original Brahman-Selfhood; therefore before the consciousness of identity with Brahman awakens, all worldly and Vaidic actions are justified." [1]

This fact is often ignored, and consequently the Vedānta is charged with fostering inaction, pessimism, leading finally to a zero-point, etc. Such objections are simply due to a misunderstanding or ignorance of passages like these.

With Śaṅkara closes our survey of the doctrine of Māyā. The theory as held to-day is in no way conflicting with the views of Śaṅkara. After having been made the object of polemics from different quarters, this theory was again revived with full force and vigour—though it has never been dead in its influence—by modern writers on the Vedānta. The same ideas of Gauḍapāda and Śaṅkara were still further elaborated, though the style of expression

[1] The spirit of such passages is exactly analogous to Kant's axiom that the transcendental ideality of the world does not exclude its empiric reality.

became more and more laboured and technical. It is not the aim of this chapter to enter into the forms in which it is exhibited in the present day. In all parts of India are still found in large numbers people who, after having thoroughly studied the various schools of Indian philosophy, acquire a peculiar attachment to the Vedānta, especially to the Advaita school of Śaṅkara. The doctrine of Māyā is the foundation-stone on which they rear the whole superstructure of their philosophy of life. The religion of the cultured Indians in modern times is identical with their philosophy, which has two aspects: *exoterically*, it is monotheistic, with the belief that the *one* Ātman manifests itself in various forms, which are taken as "means" (sādhanas) or "symbols" of attaining the Ātman—this is the lower aspect of the two; *esoterically*, monotheism has no place to hold, since it is not the final truth; the only metaphysical reality of the Absolute, *Sat*, *Cit* and *Ānanda*, is held to be no other than the Self, and all exertions are directed towards realizing this very fact. The conception of Māyā has comforted many a perplexed mind.

> "Ekasyānekamūrtitvaṃ
> yugapat paramātmanaḥ,
> saccidānandarūpasya
> sidhyen māyām ṛte katham." [1]

---

[1] From an unpublished MS. (*Māyāvādadarpaṇa*) lately added to the Bodleian Library, Oxford.

(*Trans.*)—

"How is it possible to explain the manifold simultaneous manifestations of the Absolute—being nothing but *Sat* (being), *cit* (intelligence) and *ananda* (bliss)—without having recourse to Māyā?"

OBJECTIONS TO THE DOCTRINE WITHIN THE VEDĀNTA

CHAPTER III

OBJECTIONS TO THE DOCTRINE WITHIN THE VEDĀNTA

AMONG the many objections that have been, from time to time, urged against the doctrine of Māyā, by Indian thinkers not belonging to Śaṅkara's school and by various other writers of the East and the West, most are based on a mere misunderstanding of the real significance and the correct attitude of the doctrine, as we propose to show presently. It is not our purpose here to take into account all such objections, first, because some of them are merely childish and destroy themselves in their very enunciation, and secondly, because it falls outside our scope. We will chiefly discuss those that lie within the sphere of the Vedānta proper, viz., those that have been raised by some of the other Vedāntic schools, and shall subsequently weigh briefly the principal theories commonly held up to-day in order to rebut the doctrine.

The Vedānta system easily divides itself into four schools. These are represented chronologically by Śaṅkara, Rāmānuja, Madhva, and Vallabha; and their four corresponding types of interpretation are known as Advaita, Viśiṣṭādvaita, Dvaita, and Śuddhādvaita. Each of these schools presents a different type of thought on the problem of the relation between the Absolute and the Universe, and each attempts to give its own interpretation of the principal passages of the Upaniṣads and of Bādarāyaṇa's Sūtras to suit its own pre-conceived plan of ideas.

The existence of these different schools *within* the Vedānta needs no apology. It is vain to expect all the Vedāntists to conform to the absolute rationalistic type of Śaṅkara, or to the theistic type of Rāmānuja, or to the other types. Variety, which is no less true of human nature than of the external world, demanded a variety in the philosophic and religious beliefs, and such diversity, at least in types or groups, will ever prevail. It is an idle dream to expect that at a certain time the world will have *one* form of religion, or will think in *one* set groove of thought. These four schools in the Vedānta represent four stages of the development of thought, which carry with them the philosophic and religious beliefs.

Our whole personality enters into the formation of our philosophic or religious systems, and each of us accepts the one and rejects the other in so far as it is in harmony or otherwise with his cognitive experiences or general interests. The psychological process of selection or choice is ever going on in our every-day life in all its activities. Hence it is not in any way a drawback in the Vedānta that it split itself up into four systems. This analysis was essential for a final synthesis.

In tracing the development of the conception of Māyā, we have already described in brief the main features of Śaṅkara's school. To recapitulate very briefly, we may add that the whole of it centres round the theory of Māyā. Hence its characteristics may be summed up as—

1. That the only true existence is that of Brahman.
2. That Brahman is identical with the Ātman.
3. That the universe is *Māyā*, having only a phenomenal or relative existence.

Max Müller seems to have been a little surprised, judging by his observations on Śaṅkara: "The entire complex or phenomenal existence is considered as true so long as the knowledge of Brahman and the Self of all has not arisen, just as the phantoms of a dream are considered to be true until the sleeper awakes" (ii. 1. 14), and says, "But it is very curious to find that, though Śaṅkara looks upon the whole objective world as the result of nescience, he nevertheless allows it to be real for all practical purposes (vyavahārārtham.")[1] But as we have already pointed out above, there is nothing to be surprised at in this conception. That was the only way one could reconcile the seeming reality of the world with the idea of the absolute reality. To deprive the

[1] Max Müller, *Six Systems of Indian Philosophy*, 1899, p. 202.

world totally of all relative reality, even for practical purposes, would be to propose a doctrine that would soon destroy itself, since it will not in any way explain the problem but will simply ignore it. Moreover, in this respect, Śaṅkara's views were exactly similar to those of Kant, who appeared on the world's stage about 1,000 years later. Kant, too, while strongly inveighing against the Dogmatism and Scepticism of his times, by a thorough-going critical analysis of Reason itself came to the independent conclusion that the world, qualified as it is by Time, Space, and Causality, has no metaphysical reality, but none the less is an appearance, i.e., is empirically real. We hold that whatever other weaknesses there may have been in Kant's system, his point was true beyond question. Many Hegelians of modern times have come forward with a well-arrayed attack against the fundamental doctrines of Kant, but unfortunately they have started with gratuitous premises and consequently their criticisms have mostly missed the mark.[1] Kant's "Things-in-Themselves" seem to them to stand opposed to phenomena, and so supposing a cleavage between the two worlds they infer that it is impossible to bring these two into relation. The same criticism has been preferred against Śaṅkara's conception

[1] We refer, e.g., to the works of T. H. Green (see *Prolegomena to Ethics*, ch. i.), Prichard (Kant's *Theory of Knowledge*, chap. on "Things-in-Themselves"), and many others.

of Nirguṇa Brahman (unqualified Absolute, corresponding to Kant's "Noumena" or Schopenhauer's "Will") and Saguṇa Brahman (qualified Absolute, the Īśvara,[1] corresponding to Kant's "Phenomena," or the Vedāntic idea of Māyā, or Schopenhauer's fundamental conception of the unreality of the world, when he says, "Die Welt ist meine Vorstellung.")[2]

This short digression is meant simply to point out that Śaṅkara's concession of "phenomenal" reality was not due to any aberration of his thought, but quite consonant with even the result of the modern critical philosophy of Kant and others. The point has been worked out in some detail by Deussen in his *Elemente der Metaphysik.*

As we are now concerned with the examination of the main objections to the Māyā theory, it is needless to dwell longer on its constructive side. We now give a summary of the other three schools in the Vedānta, before dealing with the objections.

The Rāmānujas represent the *theistic* school of the Vedānta. They worship Viṣṇu as their Brahman, in opposition to Śaṅkara's Nirguṇa Brahman, and, denying that the deity is void of form or quality, regard him as endowed with all good and auspicious qualities, and with a two-fold form: the supreme spirit (Paramātmā, or cause), and the gross one (the

[1] The word *Īśvara* is used in a pantheistic sense, such as would regard the whole world as pervaded by Īśvara, or a manifestation of Him, or His *body* as it were.

[2] Cf. Schopenhauer, *Die Welt als Wille und Vorstellung.*

effect, the universe, or matter). Their doctrine is consequently known as *Viśiṣṭādvaita*, or the doctrine of Unity with attributes.[1] Mādhava[2] sums up the tenets of Rāmānuja in the formula—" Three categories are established, as soul, not-soul, and Lord ; or as subject, object, and Supreme Disposer."[3]

Rāmānuja himself has furnished us with a summary of his main teachings in the introduction to his *Vedāntadīpa*. He starts with what he calls the three primary and ultimate certainties known to philosophy, viz.—

1. *God* (Hari). Universal Soul, personal, and intelligent.

2. *Soul* (cit). Individual, intelligent.

3. *Matter* (acit). Non-intelligent.

Each of these three entities is distinct from the other : God, the Supreme Soul of the Universe, is distinct from the individual soul, which again is distinct from non-intelligent matter. This difference is intrinsic and natural. The relation between God and the universe (matter and soul) is that of cause and effect. Matter and soul form the *body of God*, which in its *subtle* condition is the universe in its causal state, and in its *gross* condition the created universe itself. The individual soul enters into

[1] See Wilson, *Religious Sects of the Hindus*, London, 1861, vol. i., p. 43.

[2] Cf. *Sarvadarśanasamgraha*, Bibl. Ind., Calc., 1858, p. 46, ff.

[3] Cf. *Sarvadarśanasamgraha*, Trans. Cowell and Gough, 1882, p. 66. Deussen, *Geschichte der Philosophie*, iii., p. 261.

matter, and thereby makes it live; and, similarly, God enters into matter and soul and gives them their powers and their peculiar characters. The universe without God is exactly analogous to matter without soul.[1]

Brahman (which is identified with Hari in this system) is regarded as having *svagatabheda*, i.e., differences within itself in its threefold aspects referred to above. It is imagined to be like a tree, which, though *one*, has differences *within* itself in the shape of its branches, etc.

Madhva (also known as Ānandatīrtha and Pūrṇaprajña[2]), in the thirteenth century, proposed another system in the Vedānta, which he called the *Dvaita*. It is so called because he believed in the *duality* of ultimate principles, which he named the *independent* and the *dependent*. Difference was a real entity in itself. The relation of the individual to God, the Supreme Lord, was that of a slave and master: the latter was the former's object of obedience. Māyā is only the will of the Lord (Viṣṇu). The grace of Viṣṇu is won only through the knowledge of his excellence, not through the knowledge of non-duality. The whole world was manifest from the body of Viṣṇu.[3]

[1] Cf. Rāmānuja's *Śrībhāṣya*, trans. Raṅgācārya and Varadarāja, Madras, 1899. "Analytical Outline," p. 1.

[2] See Mādhava, *Sarvadarśanasaṃgraha*, ch. v.

[3] "Viṣṇor dehāj jagat sarvam āvirāsīt"—Wilson, *Religious Sects*, i., p. 144, note.

Vallabha, the founder of another Vaiṣṇava school of the Vedānta, flourished in the fifteenth century and taught a non-ascetic view of religion, deprecating all kinds of self-mortification, which, he said, destroyed the body in which there lives a spark of the Supreme Spirit. According to him, the highest reality was Kṛṣṇa, exempt from all qualities [1] eternal, self-sufficient, and the supreme soul of the world. The creation of the world was by a process of evolution and involution. "Kṛṣṇa being alone in the *Goloka*," as Wilson [2] says, "and meditating on the waste of creation, gave origin to a being of a female form endowed with the three *guṇas*, and thence the primary agent in creation. This was Prakṛti or Māyā." This account of Wilson is too scrappy and vague. As a matter of fact, there is a very scanty literature on the teachings of Vallabha. The Sarvadarśanasaṃgraha has no place for it, and even Deussen, following closely the plan of this book, omits it altogether from his *Geschichte der Philosophie*. Max Müller too is quite silent on the subject. We shall not give here any detailed account of Vallabha's doctrines, but we must state their essentials in so far as they affect the general conception of Māyā.

[1] Hence the name of the system as *Viśuddhādvaita*. Vallabha held that Kṛṣṇa was devoid of all qualities, while Rāmānuja had alleged before his times that Viṣṇu possessed all auspicious qualities.

[2] *Religious Sects of the Hindus*, vol. i., p. 123.

Vallabha was preceded in his line of thought by Nimbārka and Viṣṇuswāmī. He attempted to purify the viśiṣṭādvaita of Rāmānuja and others. He said it was a contradiction in terms to suppose with Rāmānuja that Brahman—all *cit*, intelligence—should be in inseparable union with *acit* (non-intelligent matter, *jaḍa*). Brahman is *sat*, *cit*, and *ānanda*; exhausts the possibility of all *being*, and *becomes* whatever it *wills* by the evolution (āvirbhāva) and involution (tirobhāva) of its properties. Whereas Śaṅkara explains the phenomena of the universe by *adhyāsa*, Rāmānuja by qualitative and inherent differences in Brahman, Madhva by manifestation of Brahman's body, Vallabha does so by the process of evolution and involution of Brahman.

After this very brief summary of the chief doctrines of the schools within the Vedānta, we come to Rāmānuja's criticism of the theory of Māyā. This is embodied in his greatest work, *The Śrībhāṣya*, a commentary on Bādarāyana's Brahmasūtras. His exposition of the first Sūtra occupies the largest space in his treatise, and this criticism appears under the same division.[1] Rāmānuja brings seven charges against the doctrine of Māyā. We reproduce the gist of each, in order, with a criticism of our own.

1. *The charge of Āśrayānupapatti.*

What is the *āśraya* (seat) of Māyā (or avidya)? Residing in what does it produce illusion? Surely

[1] See *Śrībhāṣya*, trans. Raṅgācārya and Varadarāja, Madras, 1899, pp. 156–241

not in the individual self, because the selfhood of the individual self is itself projected by *avidyā*; neither could it reside in Brahman, since He has the essential nature of self-luminous intelligence, and is thus opposed to *avidyā* (ignorance).

Criticism.—This objection rests upon a two-fold misinterpretation.—In the first place, Rāmānuja starts with the idea that Māyā (or Avidyā) is something *real,* and consequently demands a *seat* for this "illusion" or "ignorance." *Avidyā* is decidedly not a reality: it is only the negation of *vidyā,* or the obscuration of it. As the fire is latent in the wood, so is our godly nature, our spiritual principle, hidden by the *upādhis,* In the second place, Rāmānuja makes an unwarranted differentiation between Brahman and the individual soul. In stating the position of the Advaitin he has no right to colour it with his own conceptions. We, after Śaṅkara, do not admit such a difference between the two. Brahman becomes the individual soul only by *upādhis,* i.e., self-imposed limitations of *manas,* ten senses, subtle body, Karma, etc. These *upādhis* may figuratively be spoken of as limiting the Ātman and resolving it into the two aspects of the Highest Ātman (Brahman) and the individual Ātman. If, therefore, we are pressed by Rāmānuja to state the *residence* of Avidyā, we may meet him by saying that it must, if at all conceived as such, reside in the *upādhis*—the mind (manas), the senses, etc. As a matter of fact, this demand of Rāmānuja seems to be unjustifiable and inadmissible. It wholly rests upon his supposition of the *reality* of *Avidyā*.

2. *The Charge of Tirodhānānupapatti.*

The supposed "ignorance" cannot, as maintained by its upholders, conceal Brahman, whose essential nature is self-luminosity. The concealment of luminosity means either (*a*) the obstruction of the origination of luminosity, or (*b*) the destruction of existing luminosity. But as it is held that the luminosity of Brahman is incapable of being a *produced* thing, the concealment of luminosity must mean the *destruction* of luminosity, which, in other words, amounts to the destruction of the essential nature of Brahman.

Criticism.—This objection is based upon Rāmānuja's losing hold of the real position of the upholders of Māyā. Our "ignorance" is merely *negative*. It has no positive existence to be able to conceal anything else in the strict sense. Brahman is ever the same in its splendour and luminosity, but we fail to see it only through our own *avidyā*, which can, therefore, in no way be said to be able to conceal Brahman in the sense of destroying its luminosity. In the same way, if a follower of Rāmānuja were to ask Kant, "Why do we not see the thing-in-itself (das 'Ding-an-sich')?" he would at once reply, "Because between that and ourselves are the intellectual forms (*upādhis*) of Time, Space, and Causality." Thus we are not explaining away the difficulty pointed out by Rāmānuja when we say that we deny the concealment (tirodhāna) of Brahman by ignorance (avidyā).

3. *The Charge of Svarūpānupapatti.*

What is the essential nature of *Avidyā* ? As long as it is a thing at all, it must either have the nature of reality or of unreality. But it is not admitted to be a reality ; [1] and it cannot be an unreality, for, as long as a *real* misguiding error, different from Brahman Himself, is not admitted, so long it is not possible to explain the theory of illusion. If Brahman Himself have the character of the misguiding error, then, owing to his eternity, there would be no final release to the individual self.

Criticism.—The whole difficulty is purely factitious. Certainly we do not admit the reality of Māyā, but at the same time we do not hold that it is unreal from the empirical standpoint as well. Empirically it is *sat* (existing) : the world *is*, but it is *Māyā.* Rāmānuja is too anxious and tactful to corner us by his dilemmas. But as a rule these dilemmas have one of the two horns already broken, since he generally starts with self-assumed premises, and draws his own inferences from them, most logically, of course.

The question as to what is the *cause* of Māyā is, in the sense in which it is asked, an illegitimate one.

[1] Here Rāmānuja rightly understands the standpoint, but at once again makes a great confusion and becomes inconsistent when criticizing the theory on the basis of the assumed *reality* of Māyā.

Causality is the general law in the world (in Māyā), but it has no warrant to transcend itself and ask, "What is the cause of Māyā ?" The category only applies within the phenomenal world, and at once breaks down when stretched out of it. Everything within Māyā has a cause, but Māyā has no cause. The same fact would be stated by Kant in the words "Causality is the universal law of the *empirical world*". Hence the question as to causality being meaningless in the present context, we are not obliged to answer it.

Again, when Rāmānuja suggests that "as long as a *real* misguiding error, different from Brahman, is not admitted, so long it is not possible to explain the theory," the suggestion seems to us to convey hardly any meaning, since the moment we grant a *real* existence to Māyā, our whole theory falls with it ; a real dualism between the two realities (facing each other) will be at once created, and this will in no way afford even the slightest explanation of the theory. We wonder how Rāmānuja himself would try to explain the theory even on these dualistic premises. The whole of this charge, therefore, is imaginary and futile.

4. *The Charge of Anirvacanīyatvānupapatti.*

The Advaitins says that Māyā is *anirvacanīyā*, i.e., incapable of definition, because it is neither an entity (*sat*) nor a non-entity (*asat*). To hold such a view is impossible. All cognitions relate to entities or non-entities ; and if it be held that the object of a cognition has neither the positive characteristics of an entity nor the negative characteristics of a non-entity, then all things may become the objects of all cognitions.

Criticism.—This difficulty is couched in a very clever and catchy way. Yet the whole rests on a misconception, viz., the want or perceiving clearly what the "*tertium comparationis*" is in each case. *Sat* and *asat* sound two contradictory conceptions, and to say that a thing ("an object of cognition") is neither *sat* nor *asat* is not to say anything about it at all. But the thing is thought of in two wholly different aspects, and the *tertium comparationis* is not common to both.

Māyā, we say, is neither *sat* nor *asat*, neither an "entity" nor a "non-entity." It is not *sat*, since the Ātman alone is real, and it is not *asat*, since it *appears* at least, or in other words, maintains itself as an *iva* ("as it were"). Where is the contradiction now? Does not this very fact allow us to speak of Māyā as something mysterious, incapable of a strict definition?

5. *The charge of Pramāṇānupapatti.*

Is there any means by which this curious *avidyā* is brought within the range of our cognition? It can neither be proved by perception nor by inference. Neither can it be established by revelation, as the scriptural passages can be explained otherwise.

Criticism.—In the light of what we have said

above this objection stands self-condemned. When we do not believe in the real existence of Māyā, what logic is there in requiring us to prove the existence of it ? If we had granted its reality, then indeed we could be called upon to name the source of its knowledge—perception, inference, revelation, etc. However, to prove the validity of our conception we do not require any marshalled arguments or formal syllogisms. It is as clear as anything, when we recall to our mind the nature of *avidyā*, which, as we have shown after Śaṅkara, is an erroneous transfer of the things and relations of the objective world to the Self in the strictest sense of the word.

Further, Rāmānuja examines a few scriptural passages, and giving them another interpretation, infers that *all* such passages can be so explained as not to corroborate the theory of Avidyā. He might draw any meaning out of the few passages he has gone into, so long as he is bent upon showing the untenableness of Māyā, but there still remains a large number of passages, among which the metaphysics of Yājñavalkya occupies a prominent place, that defy all such attempts at a forced, far-fetched and perverted interpretation.

When we know that we are in reality no other than the Absolute Spirit, and that the Ātman is the only reality ; and yet we feel that we are different from the Absolute and that the world in which we live, move and have our being, is real, to what shall we attribute this clash between our knowledge and feelings? Is it not a mystery? And what else could we say but that this is due to our ignorance, the "erroneous transference" spoken of above?

6. *The Charge of Nivartakānupapatti.*

This difficulty is in relation to the idea that the cessation of *avidyā* takes place solely by means of the knowledge which has the attributeless Brahman for its object. Brahman is not without attributes and qualities, since there are many passages which prove that He is possessed of these. Moreover, the grammatical equations, such as "*Tattvam asi*" ("That art Thou"), do not denote the oneness of any attributeless thing, they are not intended to give rise to the stultification of any illusion due to *avidyā*; but they simply show that Brahman is capable of existing in two different modes or forms. The universe is the body of which Brahman is the soul. He is Himself all the three entities—God, soul and matter. Consequently, the knowledge which has an attributeless Brahman for its object is impossible and cannot be the complete knowledge of truth; and obviously such an impossible knowledge of the oneness of the attributeless Brahman cannot be the remover of the *avidyā* postulated by the Advaitins.

Criticism.—The force of this objection lies mainly in the supposition that "Brahman is not without attributes," and it is further pointed out by Rāmānuja that many passages of the Śruti prove this thesis. In the light of Śaṅkara's Advaita, as briefly described in Chapter II, we fail to see the force of this argument. To say that there are some scriptural passages bearing out the assertion may equally be met by the counter-proposition that there are also passages countenancing the attributelessness of Brahman. If, then, both these assertions neutralize each other from the scriptural point of view, one may well ask, What then is the real trend and purport of the Vaidic thought? It seems to us that this question could not be better answered than by repeating the doctrine of Śaṅkara when he attempted to synthesize the whole of the Śruti by taking a wide conspectus of its purport. All passages which speak of the qualified Brahman may be placed under *Aparā vidyā*, while *parā* will include only those that expound the metaphysical truth as it is. Brahman may, from a lower standpoint, be conceived as "*with* attributes," but the ultimate truth remains that He is really "*without* attributes." Besides, the conception of the Absolute in the strict sense leaves hardly any room for "attributes." Impose any attributes and you at once make the Absolute "non-absolute," i.e., destroy his very nature by making *paricchinna* (limited) that which is *aparicchinna* (without limits).

Again, Rāmānuja denies that the text, "*Tat tvam asi*," denotes the oneness of the individual with the attributeless Universal, and holds that it simply brings out Brahman's capability of existing in two forms or modes. Now, this seems to us to be an ambiguous use of language. That Brahman exists in two opposite forms will be meaningless if one of the forms were not supposed to be due to Avidyā. How can a being exist in two contradictory forms? *Cit* and *acit* are two opposite notions in the system of Rāmānuja, but he has not succeeded in reconciling their existence by merely saying that they are two modes of the Absolute. To picture the universe as the body of Brahman is after all a mere analogy, which hardly makes the matter even a jot clearer. Even by investing God with all auspicious attributes, how will Rāmānuja account for the existence of evil (moral) or error (psychological)? Simply to say, as did Plato, that God is good, hence the universe must be good, is no explanation, but a mere shirking of the question. Like Plato, Rāmānuja uses many analogies and metaphors while speaking of Brahman, but the Advaitist cannot but take all these as mere *mythical* representations.

Hence, with our denial of the qualified aspect of Brahman as a metaphysical truth is linked the denial of "the impossibility of the knowledge which has an attributeless Brahman for its object."

Avidyā being like darkness is itself expelled when light comes in. *Jñāna* is the remover of *ajñāna*. As we have already pointed out above, the expression "knowledge of Brahman" is strictly inadmissible, since Brahman is itself knowledge (*Jñāna*)—of course the term being used in the higher sense of "pure consciousness."

7. *The Charge of Nivṛttyanupapatti.*

The removal of the Advaitin's hypothetical "ignorance" is quite impossible. The individual soul's bondage of "ignorance" is determined by *Karma* and is a concrete reality. It cannot therefore be removed by any abstract knowledge—but only by divine worship and grace. Moreover, according to the Advaitins the differentiation between the knower, knowledge, and the known is unreal; and even that knowledge, which is capable of removing *avidyā* has to be unreal and has to stand in need of another real removing knowledge.

Criticism.—Our struggle with *Karma* is undoubtedly real so long as our consciousness of the true nature of Brahman has not arisen. *Karma,* its determinations, and with it everything else, is supposed to be real, but only so far. We have already quoted passages from Śaṅkara where he clearly and unequivocally makes this concession, "*vyāvahāric-ally*" (i.e., from the practical or empiric point of view), as he calls it. It may therefore be called "a concrete reality," but with the explicit understanding that such a reality is after all "phenomenal." We do not hold the efficacy of *Karma* in the case of one who has attained the knowledge of Brahman; such a man, being free from all desires and motives, all springs of action, is *pari passu* beyond the control of *Karma* in so far as he is not creating any fresh and new *Karma* for himself. The laws of *Karma* are valid within the phenomenal, but in no way do they produce any *real* knowledge to the Ātman, whose very nature forbids all such bondages.

The idea of divine worship and grace may be supported for the sake of the ordinary minds unable to go round the higher path of pure knowledge. But surely the idea of grace, etc., is not an exalted conception. Truly speaking, *grace* is only possible when there is a direct and perfect communion—in other words, an "identity"—between the two forms of consciousness. This fact, too, shows that the ultimate nature of man and God is "Consciousness." So long as our ignorance is not cast away by the acquirement of "knowledge"—which alone is capable of ousting its opponent—liberation is impossible. Without such a knowledge, mere devotion or deeds will never lead one to the same goal.

As to the differentiation between the knower (jñātā), knowledge (jñāna), and the known (jñeya), we have to repeat that the distinction is certainly fictitious in the absolute sense. It is made by us and it is real for all our practical purposes. The metaphysical truth does not attempt to devour the world in its practical aspect. The knowledge removing *avidyā*—if we are at all to say "*removal*" of *avidyā*—is not unreal. Unreal knowledge cannot destroy unreality. Knowledge in the lower sense of a relation between "subject" and "object" is of course unreal, but such knowledge is unable to give a deathblow to *avidyā*. On the dawning of true knowledge the artificial distinction between "subject" and "object" vanishes. "By what shall we know the *knower* (the subject of all knowledge)?" as was so forcibly asked by Yājñavalkya.

These are in brief the seven difficulties which Rāmānuja perceived in the doctrine of Māyā. As will appear from what we have said above, Rāmānuja's criticism rests on the whole on a misunderstanding of the genuine Advaita standpoint. All through he has been treating *Māyā* as if it were a concrete reality, even perhaps existing in space, etc. We do not accuse him even because he attempted to reject Śaṅkara's premises. But we fail to see his consistency, when even on his own premises he falls short of furnishing a really adequate explanation of the relation between God and the Universe. His doctrine of divine grace, devotion, etc., is apt to appeal strongly to many Christian theologians, who will therefore naturally prefer his philosophy to that of Śaṅkara. Be as it may, to us it seems evident that Śaṅkara's analysis of Reality went much further than Rāmānuja's. The impersonal conception of the Absolute, we hold, is truly personal, if there is any real meaning in "personality." This is how we will meet those who cannot hold any such doctrine to be the ultimate if it destroys the idea of the divine personality.

Now, coming to the objections of the Pūrṇaprajñas—who hold the absolute separateness of the individual soul and Brahman—it is obvious that the general drift of their attacks must be directed against the Advaitist's doctrine of the identity of the two. The Jīva, they say, being limited (paricchinna) is distinct from Brahman. One of the followers of this school of Madhva speaks of the Advaitins in the following contemptuous and polemic fashion—

"There are certain disputants, sunk in a sea of false logic, addicted to an evil way, filled with a hundred imaginations of idle babble, deceived themselves and deceiving the world, who say, 'I am Brahman, and all this universe also is Brahman,' which is now shown to be an empty desire. If I and all this Universe were Brahman, then there would be an identity between thee and me; thy wealth, sons and wife would be mine, and mine would be thine, for there would be no distinction between us." [1]

To show the futility of such arguments it is sufficient only to state them as such. This criticism quite ignores Śaṅkara's repeated warning that the ideal unreality of the world does not deprive it of its empiric reality, and in empiric reality all the distinctions are observed. The criticism is further couched in rather crude language. We are not surprised that a misunderstanding of the Advaita standpoint may lead one to urge such silly charges against it as are embodied in the quotation just noted.

The school of Vallabha has not entered into conflict with the theory of Māyā, but it has pointed out the untenableness of Rāmānuja's standpoint. Rāmānuja, as we have seen, only qualified the origi-

[1] See *Tattvamuktāvalī* of Pūrṇānanda, trans. by Cowell (JRAS., vol. xv. part ii.), Śloka 87–88.

nal Advaita; but Vallabha thought of purifying it altogether. It could not be held that Brahman, which is all *cit*, should be in inseparable union with *acit*. This would have been a contradiction in terms, and would have soiled the doctrine of the Upaniṣads.[1] Brahman was therefore supposed to *become* by its *will*. Now, this tendency to question the validity of Rāmānuja's standpoint went so far as to keep the school of Vallabha away from discussing the theory of Māyā. While Rāmānuja made it a point to use all means at his disposal to bring the doctrine of Māyā into discredit (and so too did Madhva after him), Vallabha stood up to criticize Rāmānuja. That is why we do not find any special charges preferred by him against "Māyā." Of course, this does not mean that he endorsed the theory, but simply that he did not meddle with the right or wrong of the question, and was content to establish his own views in reference to a criticism of Rāmānuja's. Hence we now pass on to an examination of some of the other objections, which are not raised strictly within the Vedānta.

Śaṅkara has discussed at length the controversy between the Sāṅkhya and the Vedānta. In Adhyāya i. he has established the main principles of Vedānta, and in Adhyāya ii. has attempted a thorough-going inquiry into the various objections preferred by the Sāṅkhyas (ii. 2. 1–10), Vaiśeṣikas (ii. 2. 11–17), Buddhists (ii. 218–32), Jainas (33–36), Pāśupatas (37–41),

[1] See Dvivedi, *Monism or Advaitism*, p. 104.

Pañcarātras (42–45), etc. The physico-theological proof is first taken up, and it is shown how the Pradhāna (non-intelligent matter, an equilibrium of the three guṇas) cannot evolve itself spontaneously into multiform modifications. An earthen jar though springing from clay does not itself come into existence without the co-operation of an intelligent being, viz., the potter. From the impossibility of the orderly arrangement of the world and the impossibility of activity a non-intelligent cause of the world is not to be inferred. Activity may of course belong to those non-intelligent things in which it is observed, but in every case it results from an intelligent principle, because it exists when the latter is present and not otherwise. The motive-power of intelligence is incontrovertible.

It may be objected that on the Vedāntic premises there is no room for a moving power, as in consequence of the non-duality of Brahman no motion is possible. But, says Śaṅkara, such objections have been refuted by pointing to the fact of the Lord being fictitiously connected with Māyā, which consists of name and form presented by *Avidyā*. Hence motion can be reconciled with the doctrine of a non-intelligent first cause.

We cannot enter into this question at any length, since, as we have already said, as regards the nature of Brahman as the *Cause* of the world and the possibility or otherwise of assuming any other such cause, this conception of "causality" is not tenable in the purely idealistic sense, and the moment any such category is introduced the Absolute (Brahman) is conceived as *Phenomenal* (māyopahita).

After a careful criticism of the atomic theory of the Vaiśeṣikas Śaṅkara proceeds to discuss the doctrine of the Buddhists (ii. 2. 18–32). That doctrine, as he observes, is presented in a variety of forms, due either to the difference of the views maintained by Buddha at different times, or else to the difference of capacity on the part of the disciples of Buddha. Three principal opinions may, however, be distinguished—

(1) *Realists*, who maintain the reality of everything—*Sarvāstitvavāda* (*Sautrāntikas* and *Vaibhāṣikas*).

(2) *Idealists*, who maintain the reality of thought only—*vijñānavādins* (*Yogācāras*).

(3) *Nihilists*, who maintain that everything is *śūnya* (void, unreal)—*Śūnyavādins* (Mādhyamikas).

The criticism of each of these is set forth with great perspicacity in Śaṅkara, and it is needless for us to go over the same ground again. All this bears on our subject only *indirectly*.

All the chief objections to Māyā rest upon a misconception, viz., to take it as a *reality*. Even the criticism of Thibaut in his introduction to the Vedāntasūtras (S.B.E., vol. xxxiv.) rests upon the same sort of misconception. It is exceedingly difficult to free one's mind from a theistic bias when approaching the doctrine of Māyā. In Chapter II we have attempted to show how the *idea* of Māyā existed much earlier than the *word* Māyā (in the technical sense) and that in itself is a refutation of the main thesis of scholars like Thibaut and others who suppose that the conception of Māyā was a late offshoot in the Vedānta, being specially fabricated by Śaṅkara.

On a future occasion we hope to supplement the present treatment of Māyā by an examination of the various analogies of the concept in the philosophy of the West and some other eastern countries. It may also be possible to summarize critically the views of all the other systems of Indian philosophy on the question of the relation of the Absolute to the Universe. That will be a proper occasion for recapitulating a criticism of Buddhism, Jainism, Śaṅkhya, etc.

BUTLER & TANNER
SELWOOD PRINTING WORKS · FROME